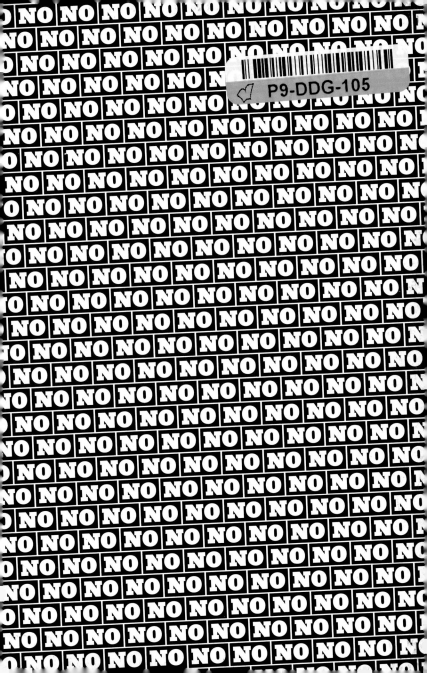

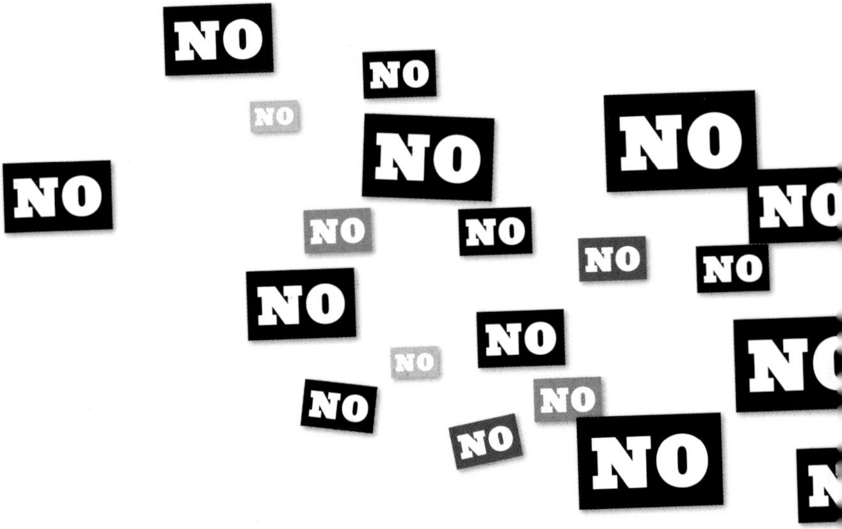
NO
NO
NO
NO
NO
NO
NO
NO
NO
NO
NO
NO
NO
NO
NO
NO
NO

GRUMPY CAT®

NO-IT-ALL

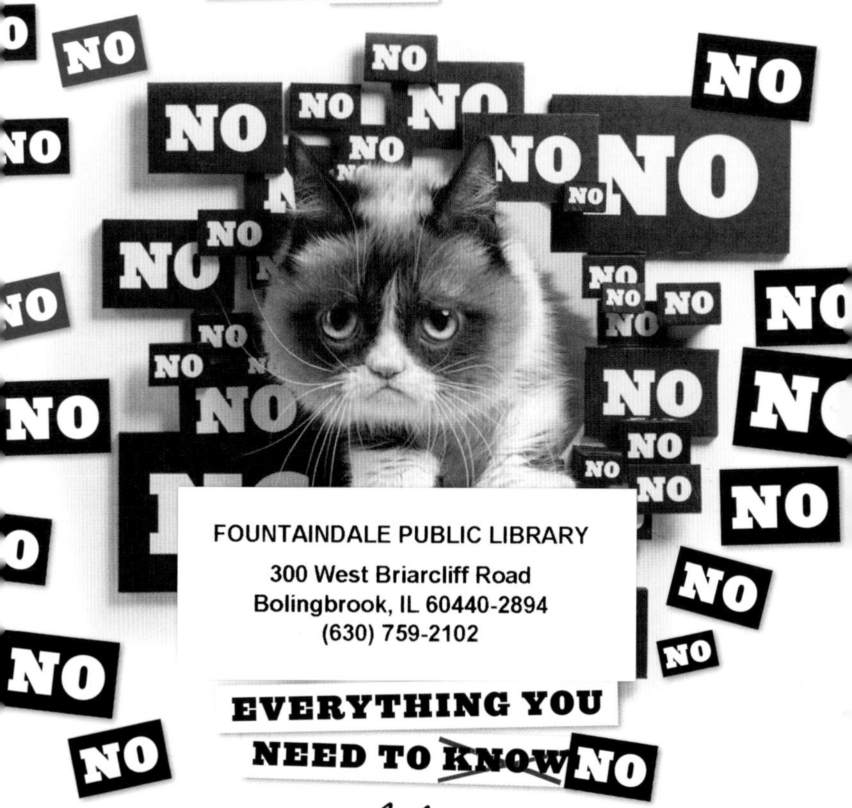

EVERYTHING YOU NEED TO ~~KNOW~~ NO

CHRONICLE BOOKS
SAN FRANCISCO

NO *Thanks to:*

Bryan, Tabatha, Chyrstal, and Elizabeth Bundesen, Ben Lashes, Heather Taylor, Kia Kamran, Julianne Freund, Molly Alward, Todd Thorson, Michael Morris, Wynn Rankin, Michelle Clair, Lia Brown, April Whitney, Albee Dalbotten, Ryan Cunningham, Liza Algar, Paul Myers, Peter Perez, Mike Adkins, Angela Bundesen, Betty Smith, Pokey, Shaggy, and Grumpy's Frienemies everywhere!

www.grumpycats.com

Library of Congress Cataloging-in-Publication Data is available.

ISBN: 978-1-4521-4968-4

Manufactured in China

MIX
Paper from
responsible sources
FSC
www.fsc.org   FSC™ C104723

STOCK IMAGE CREDITS:
p. 48-9 Dream Master / Shutterstock.com

10 9 8 7 6 5 4 3 2 1

Chronicle Books LLC
680 Second Street
San Francisco, California 94107
www.chroniclebooks.com

Dedicated to the most useful
word in the world:

NO

SAYING "YES" IS OVERRATED.

IF YOU REALLY WANT TO GET NOTHING DONE, JUST SAY ONE MAGIC WORD:

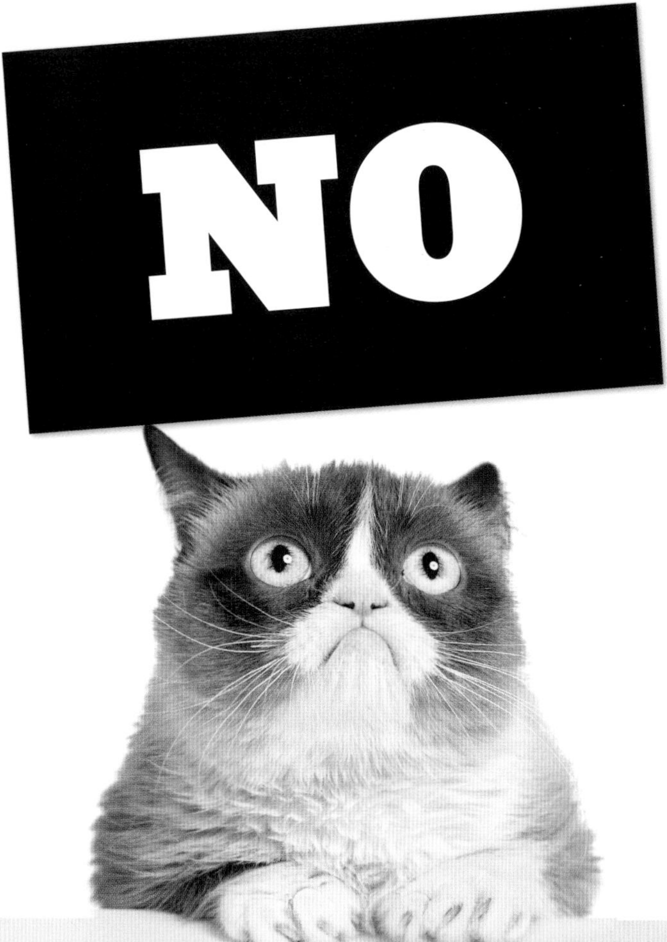
NO

THIS BOOK CONTAINS ALL OF MY LEAST FAVORITE THINGS. CONSIDER IT YOUR GUIDE TO EVERYTHING YOU NEED TO NO.

WHY NO?

WHEN YOU SAY YES

☺ **PEOPLE SMILE**

☺ **CONVERSATIONS KEEP GOING**

☺ **YOU HAVE TO DO SOMETHING**

WHEN YOU SAY NO

☹ **PEOPLE FROWN (IF YOU'RE LUCKY)**

☹ **CONVERSATIONS END**

☹ **YOU HAVE TO DO NOTHING**

WINNER: NO

NOW STOP ASKING QUESTIONS AND TAKE THE "NO-IT-ALL" OATH:

"I (STATE YOUR NAME) DO SOLEMNLY SWEAR TO SAY **NO** AND NOTHING BUT **NO** TO EVERYTHING I SEE, SO HELP ME GRUMPY CAT."

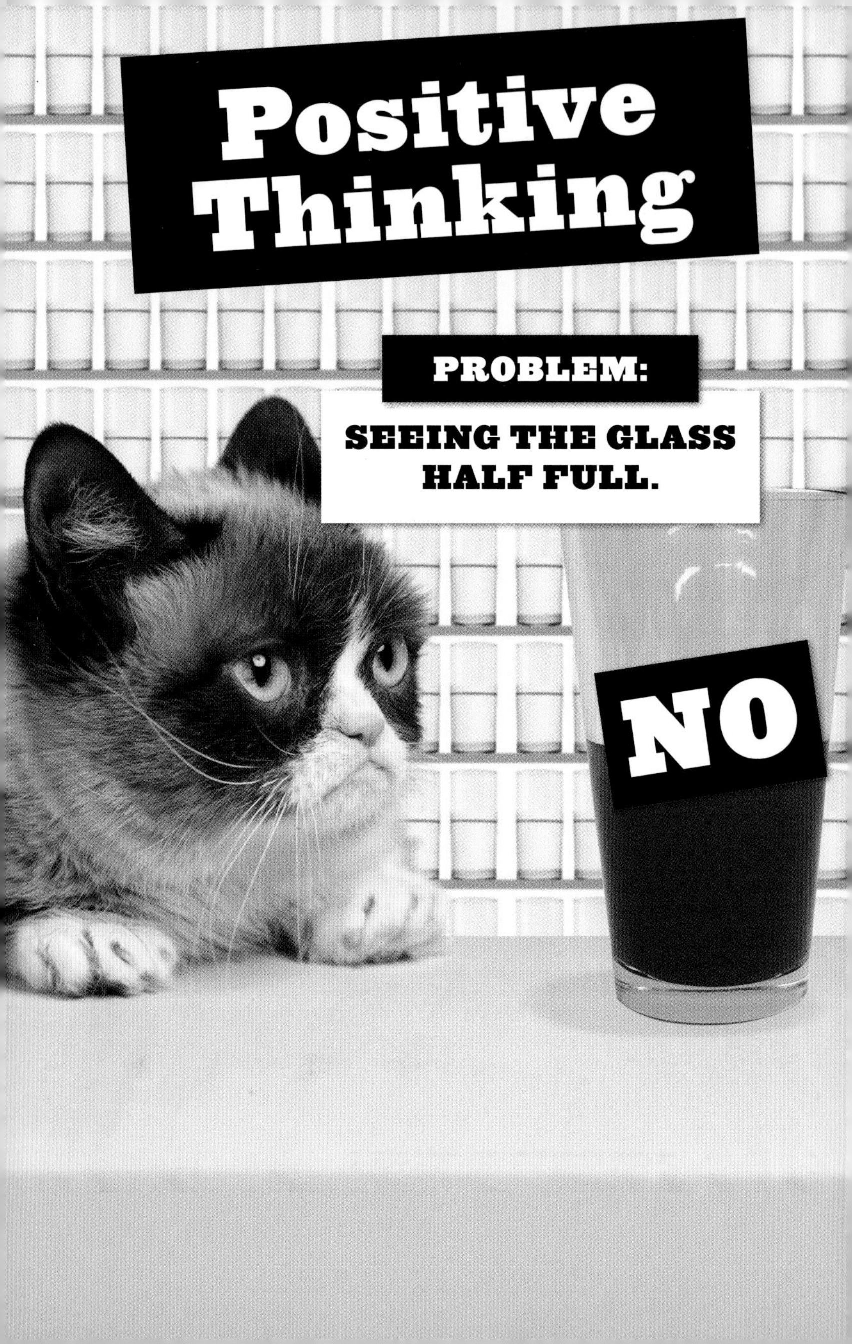
Positive Thinking
PROBLEM:
SEEING THE GLASS HALF FULL.
NO

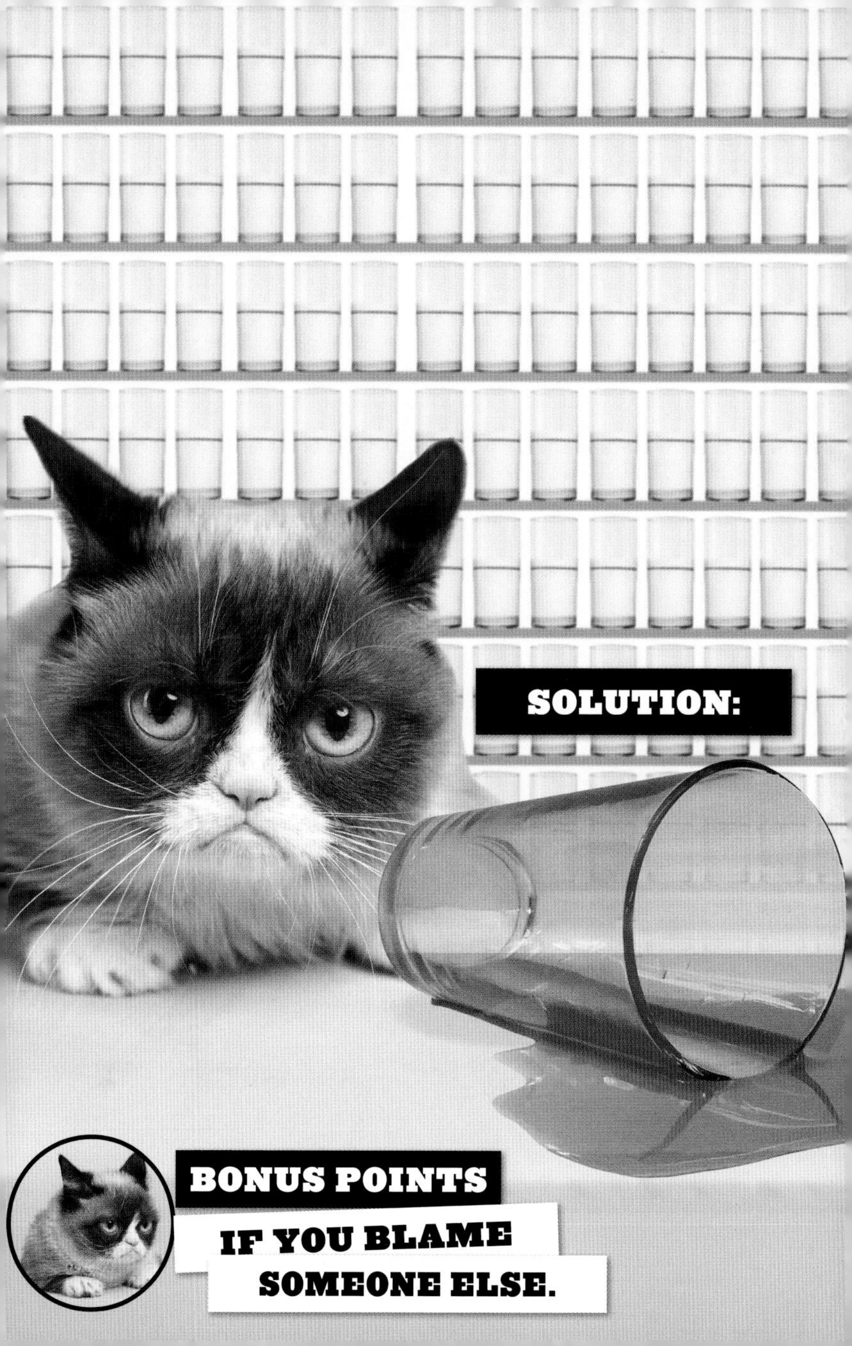
SOLUTION:
BONUS POINTS
IF YOU BLAME
SOMEONE ELSE.

Butterflies

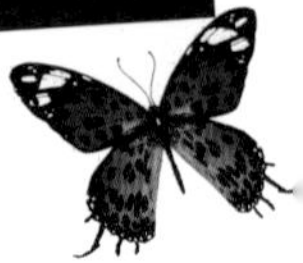

You see a wonder of nature.
I SEE A STUPID FLYING BUG SHOWING OFF.

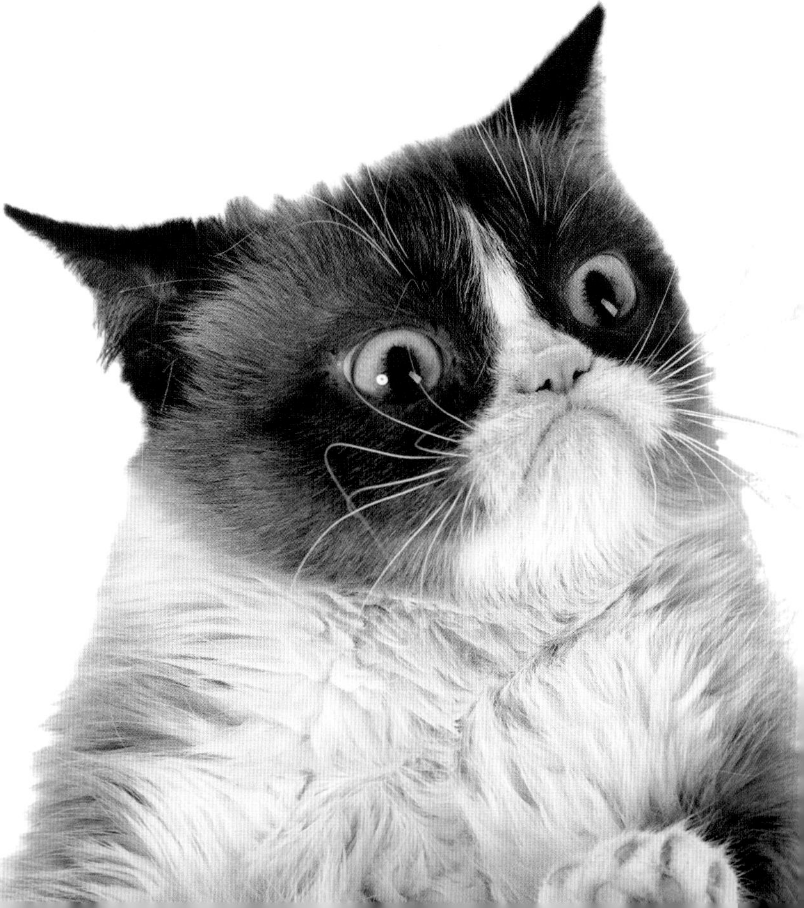

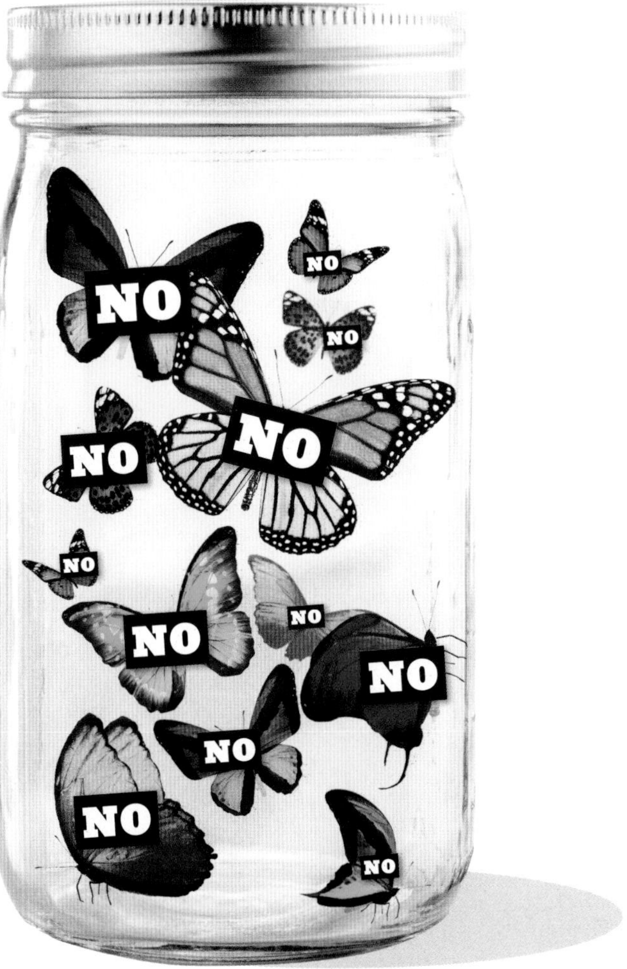
NO
NO
NO
NO
NO
NO
NO
NO
NO
NO
NO
NO
NO

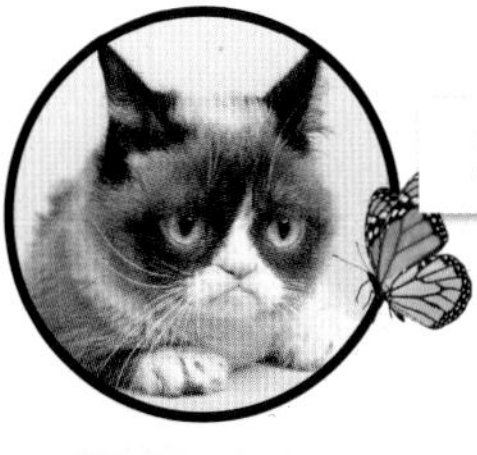

I LIKED YOU BETTER
IN THE COCOON.

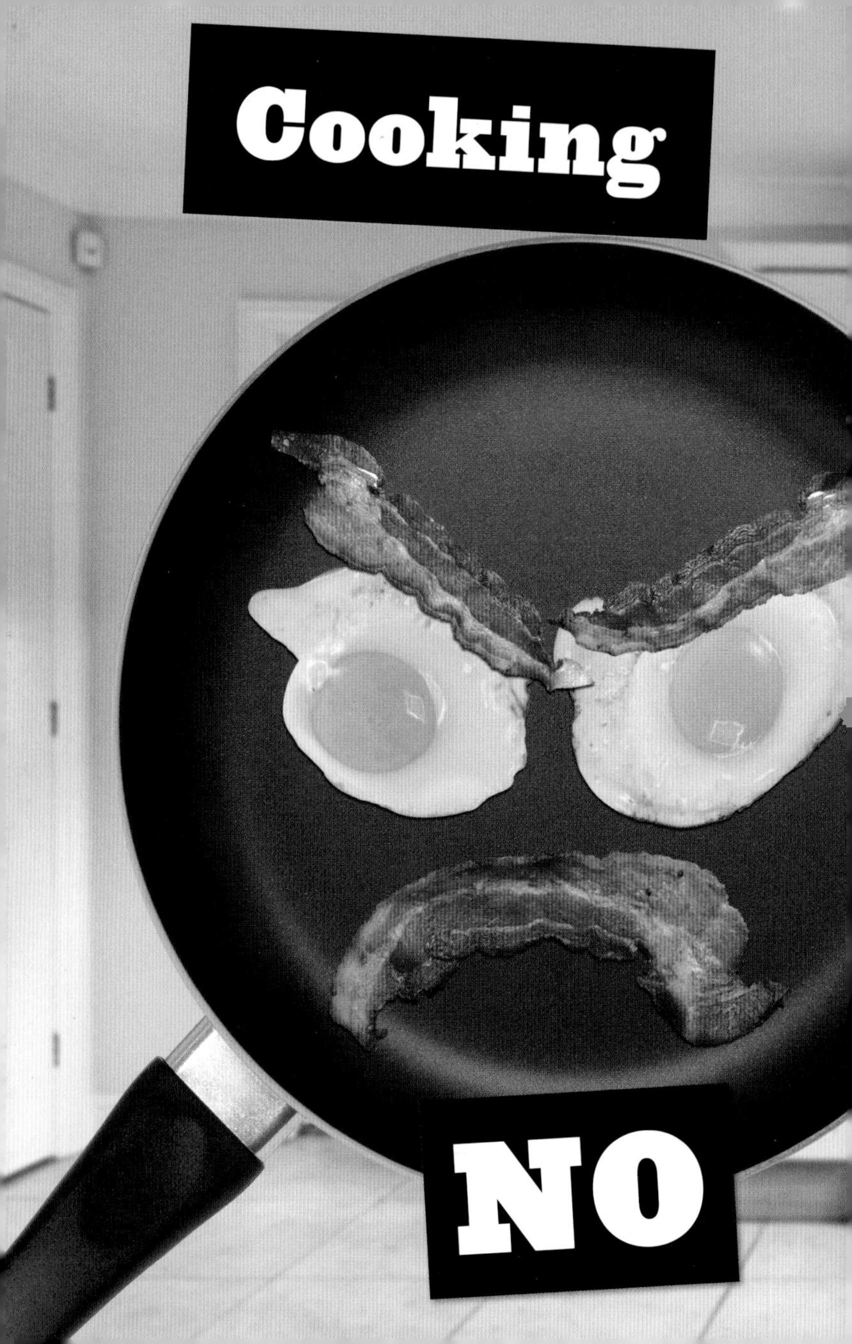
Cooking
NO

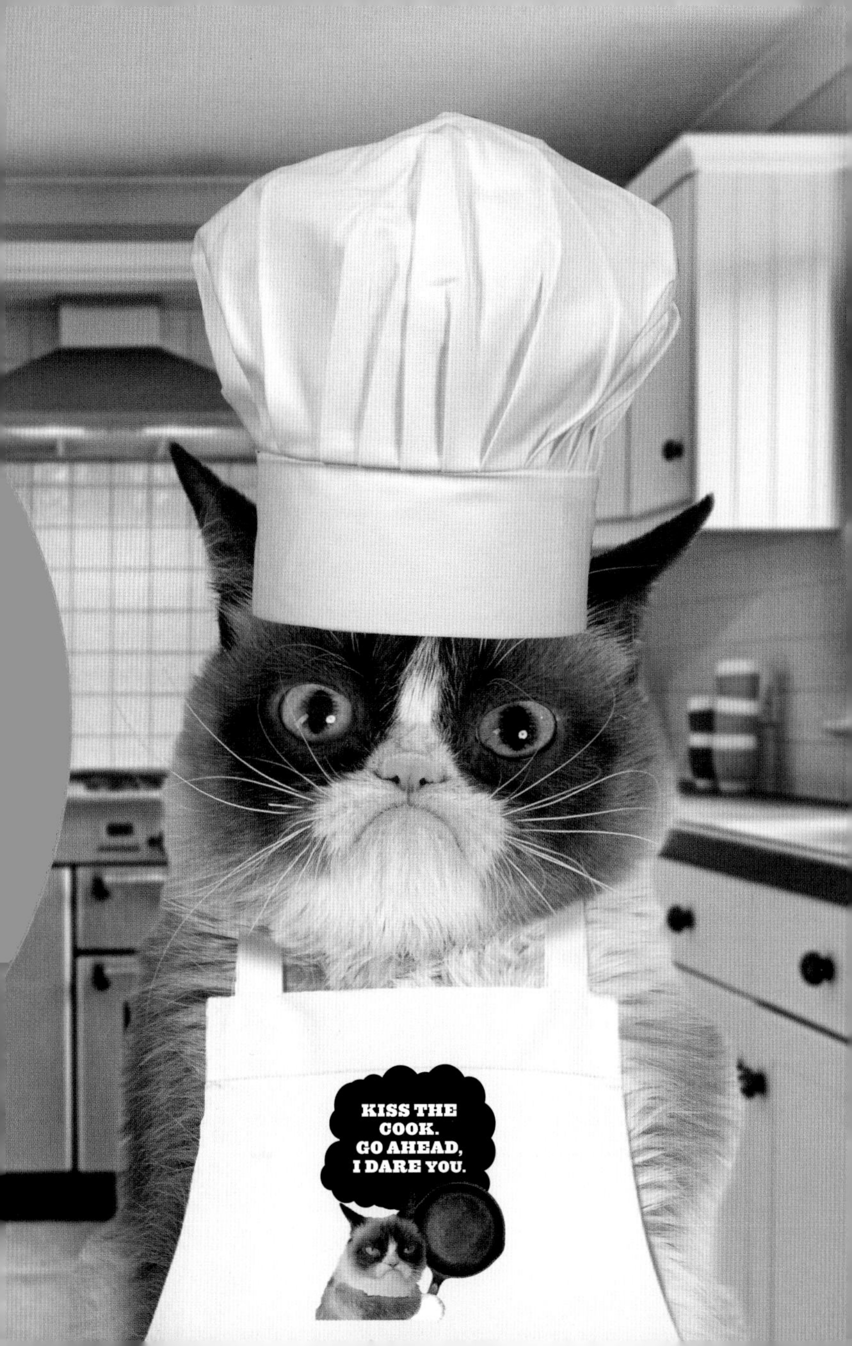
KISS THE COOK. GO AHEAD, I DARE YOU.

Flowers

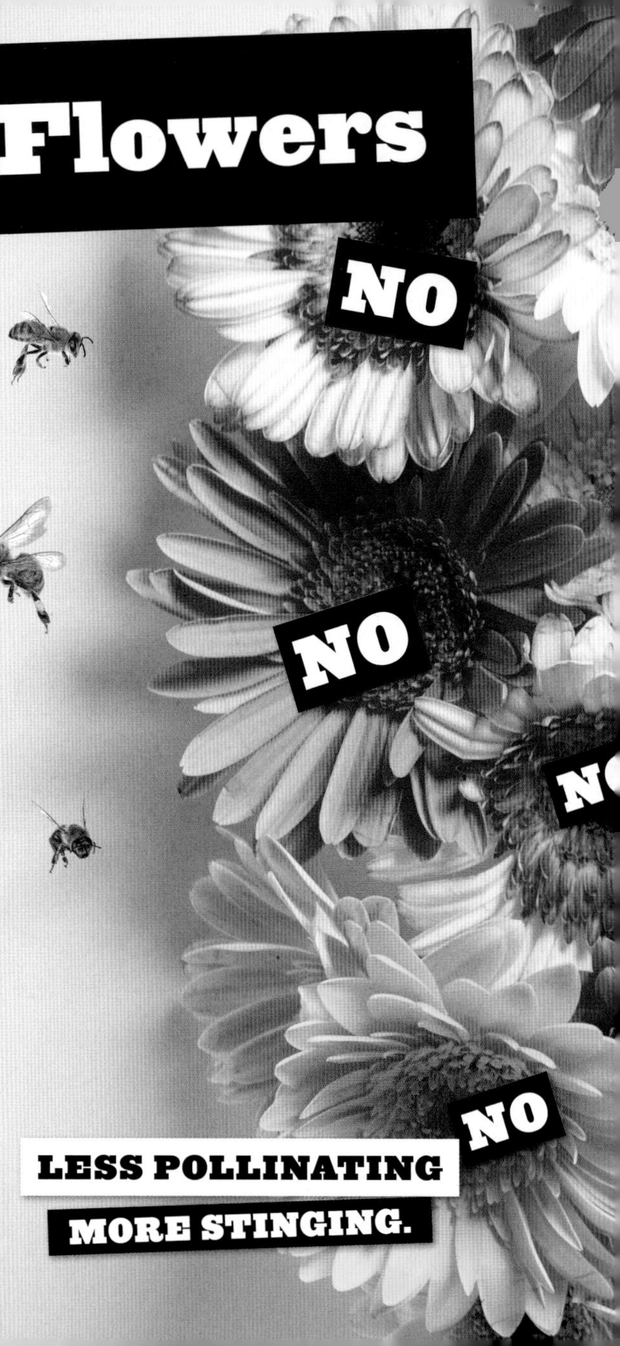
NO
NO
NO

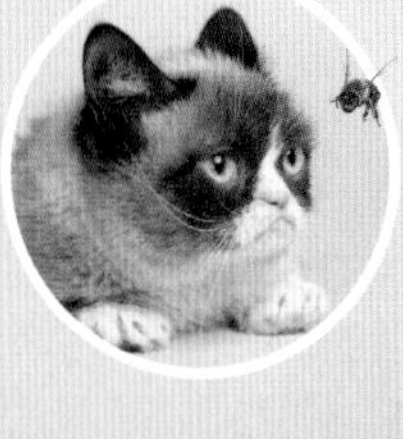

LESS POLLINATING
MORE STINGING.

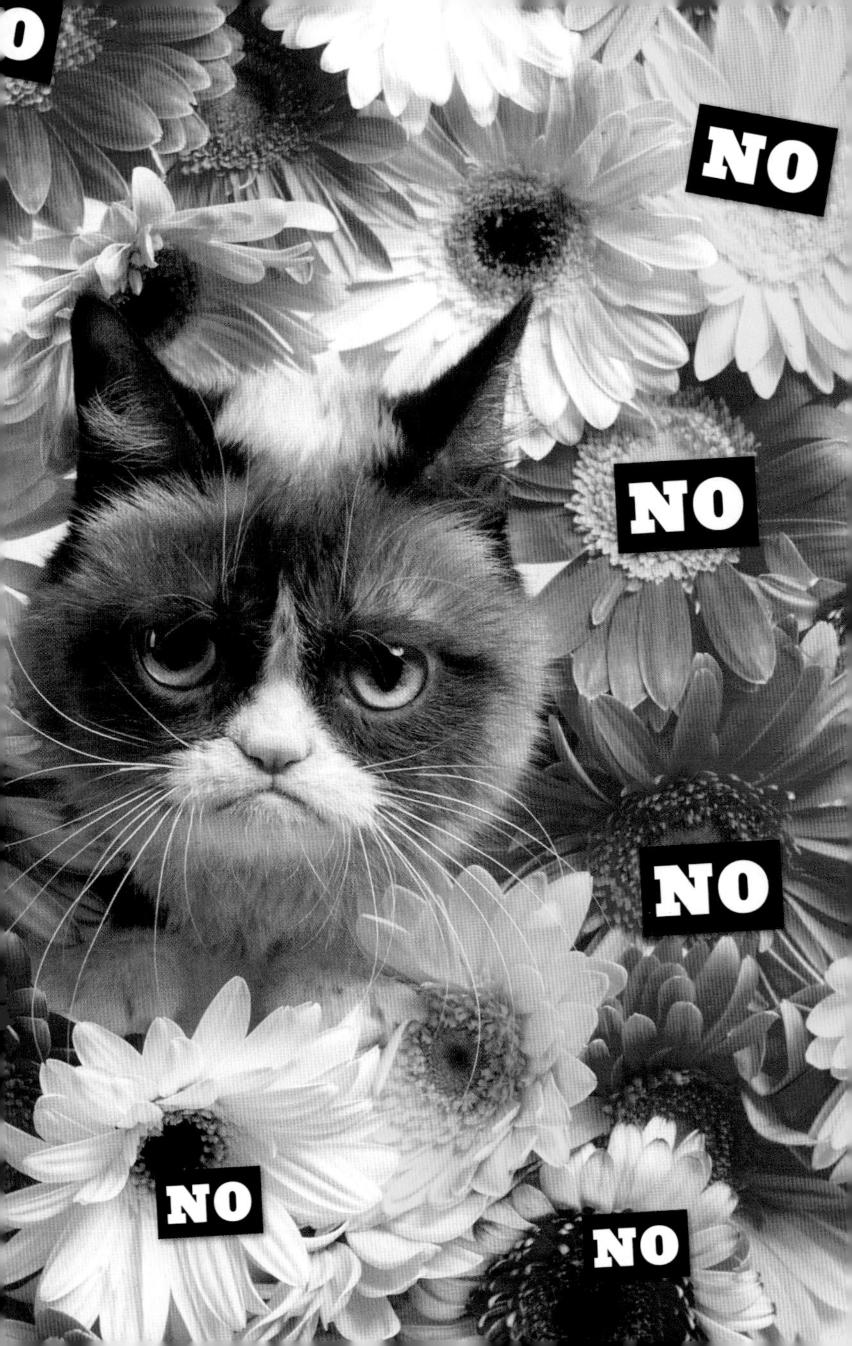

NO
NO
NO
NO
NO

Holidays

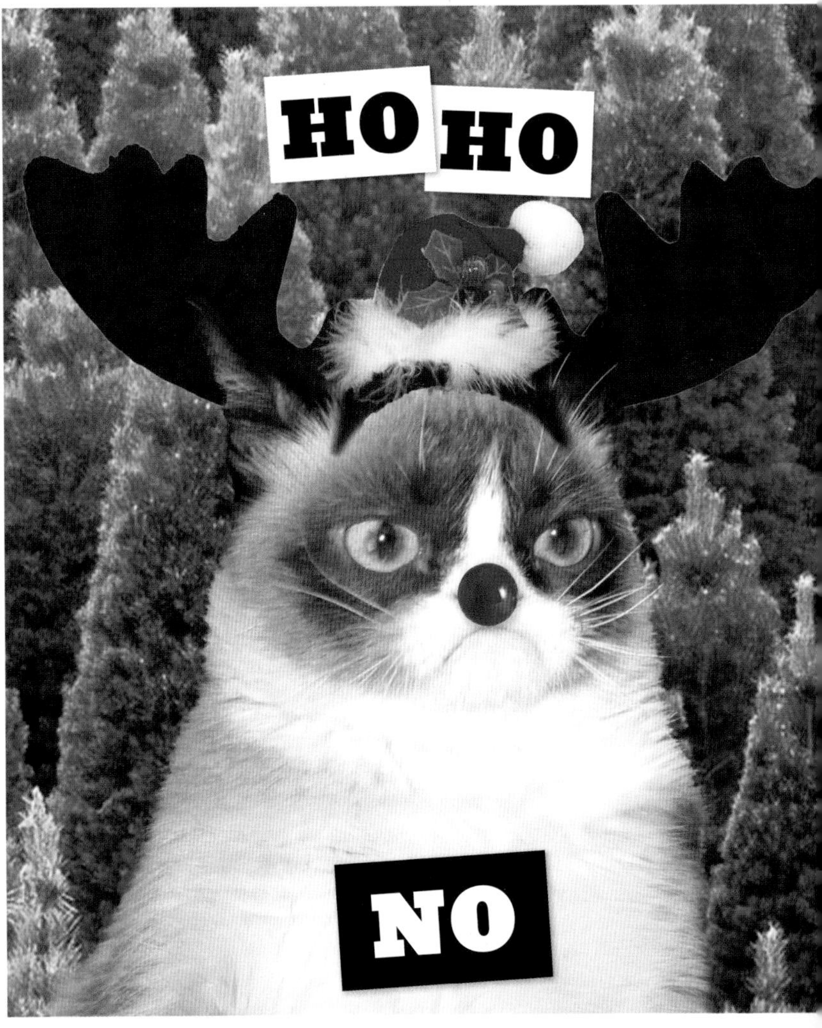
HO HO
NO

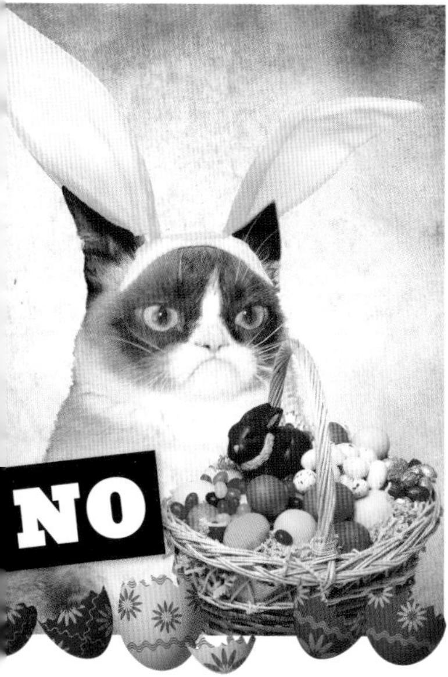
NO
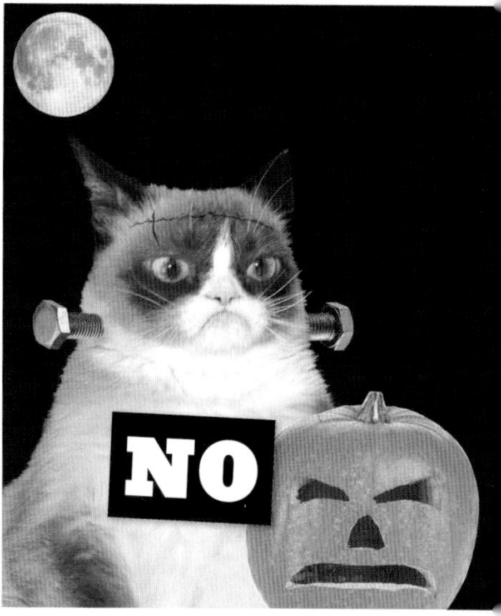
NO
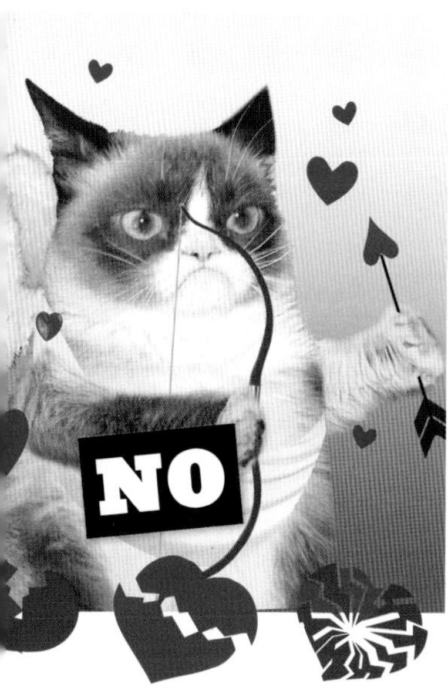
NO
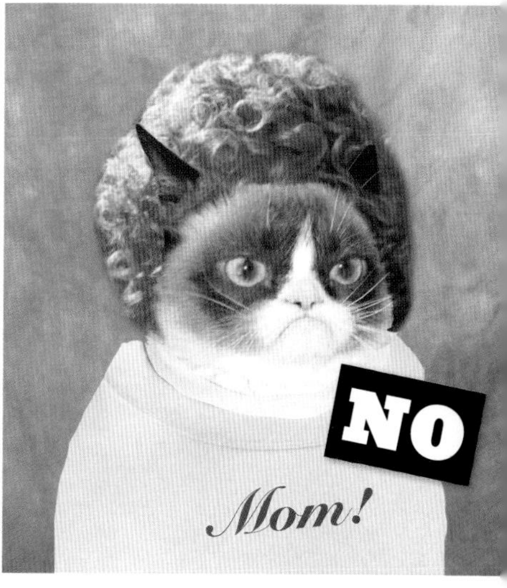
NO
Mom!

Flying

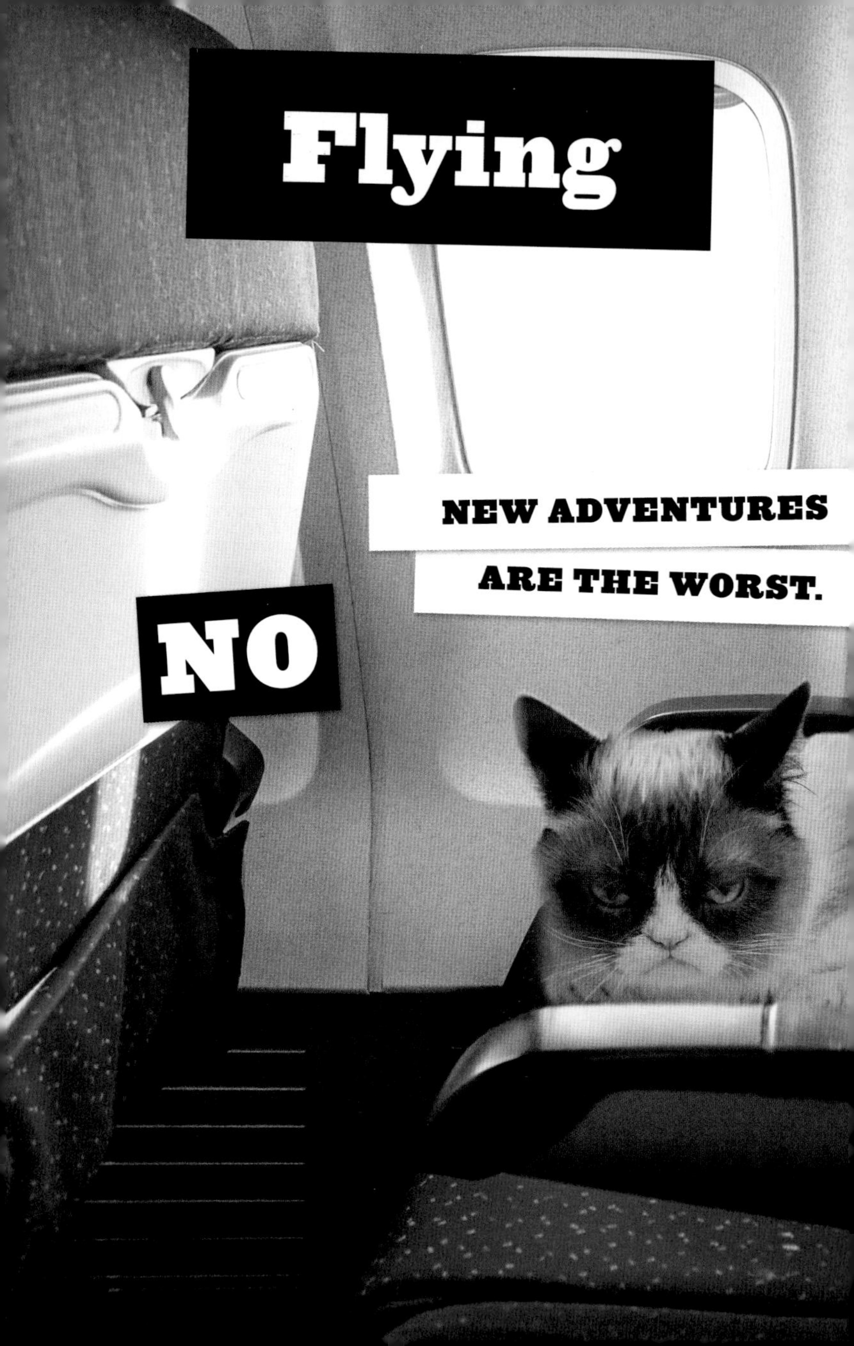

NEW ADVENTURES ARE THE WORST.

NO

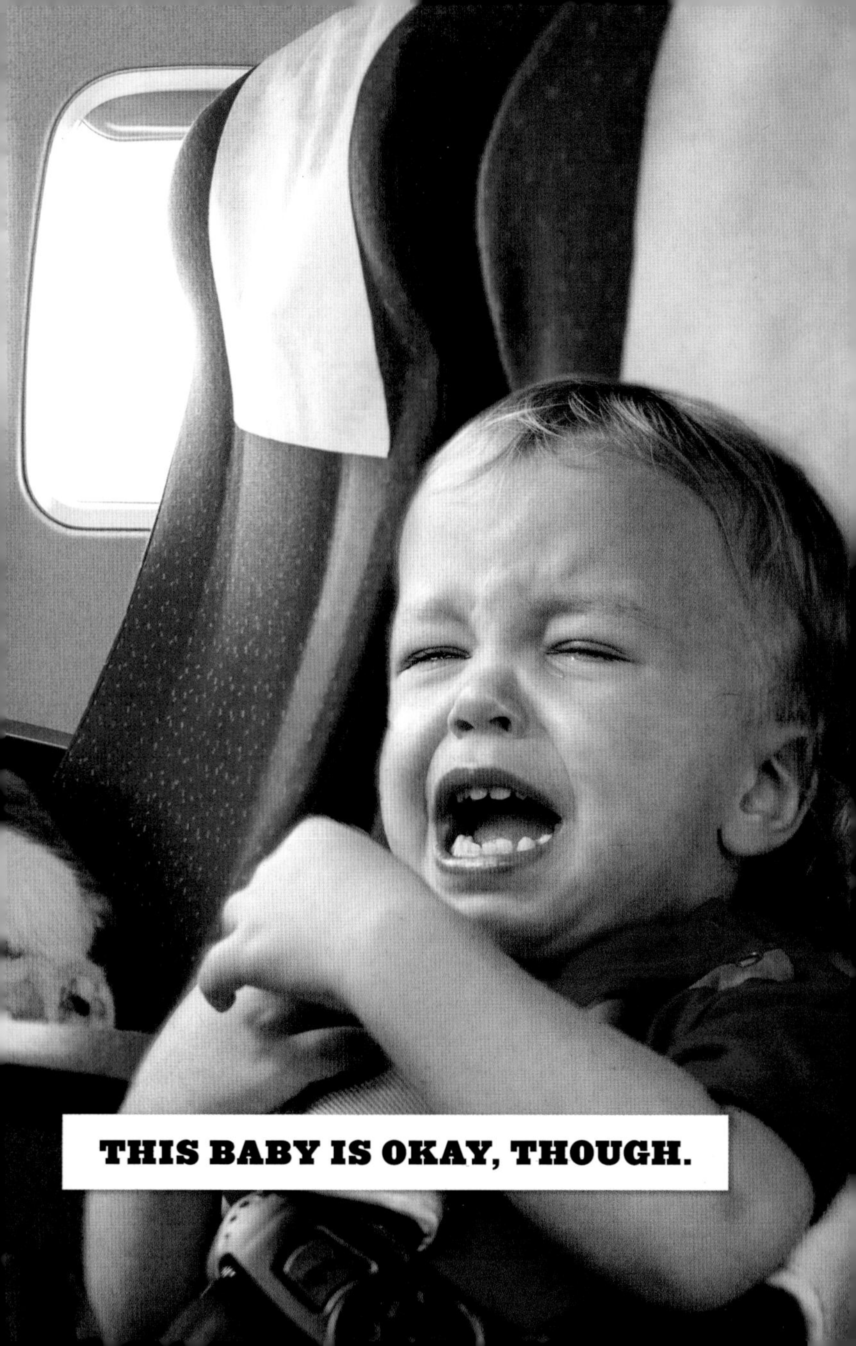

THIS BABY IS OKAY, THOUGH.

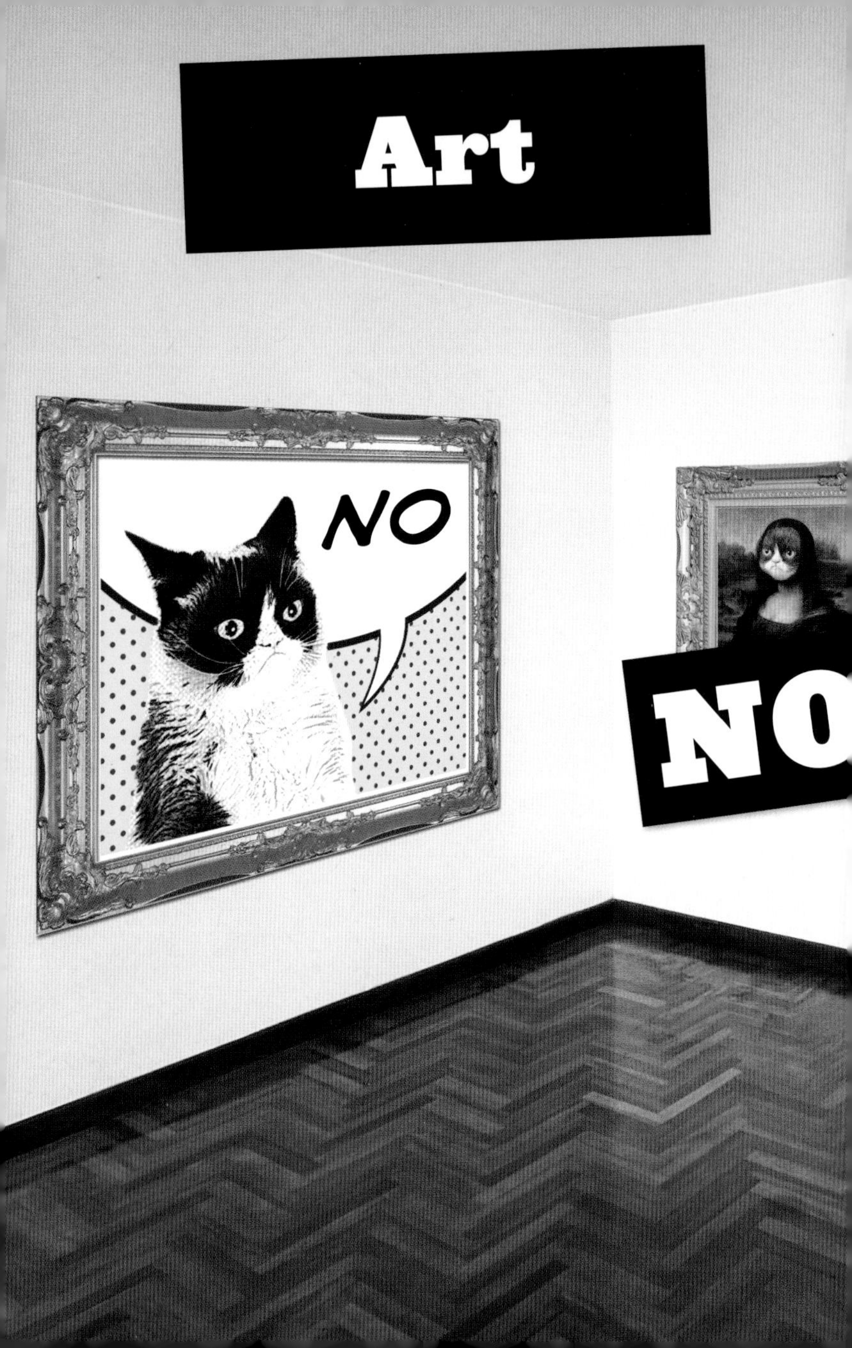
Art
NO
NO

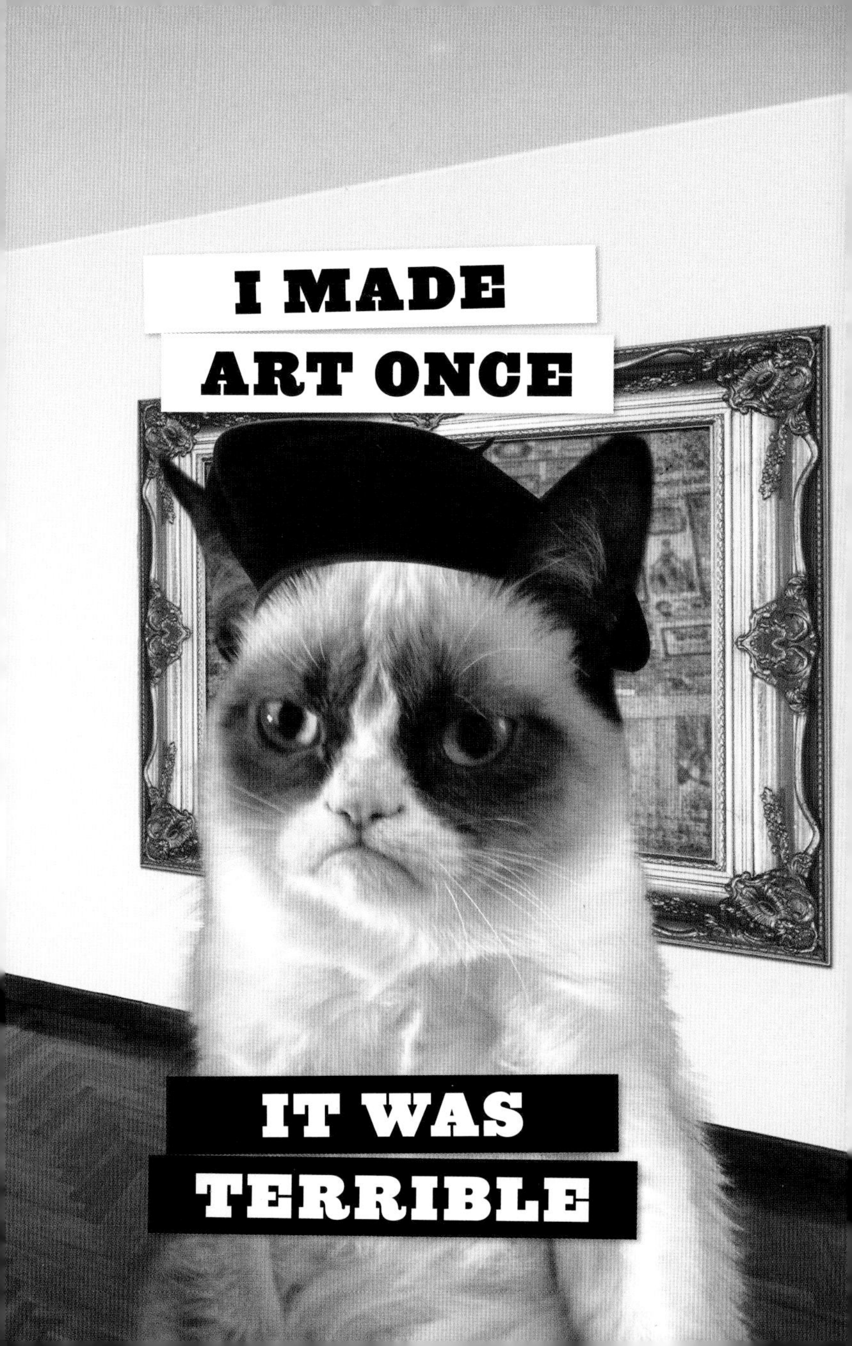
I MADE
ART ONCE
IT WAS
TERRIBLE

Amusement Parks

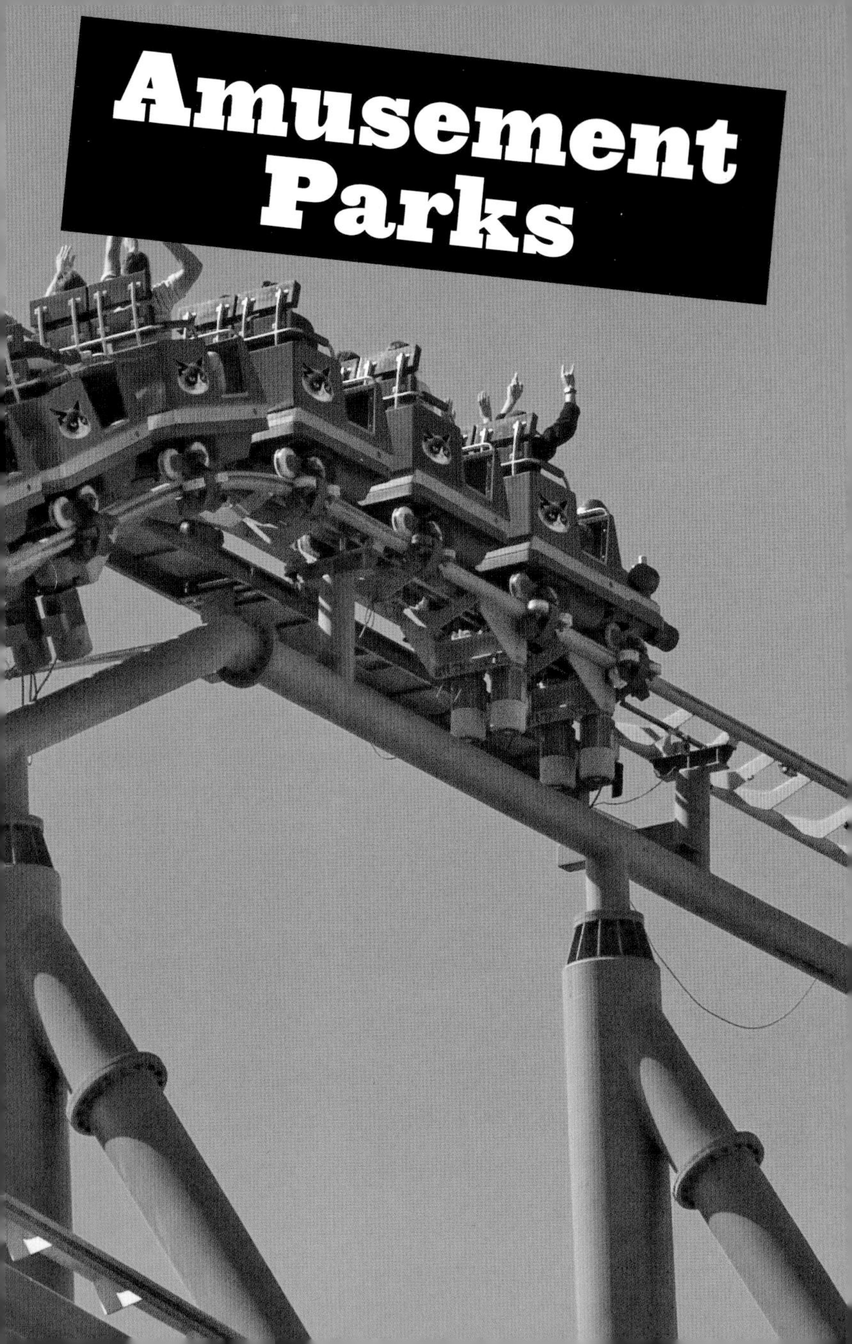

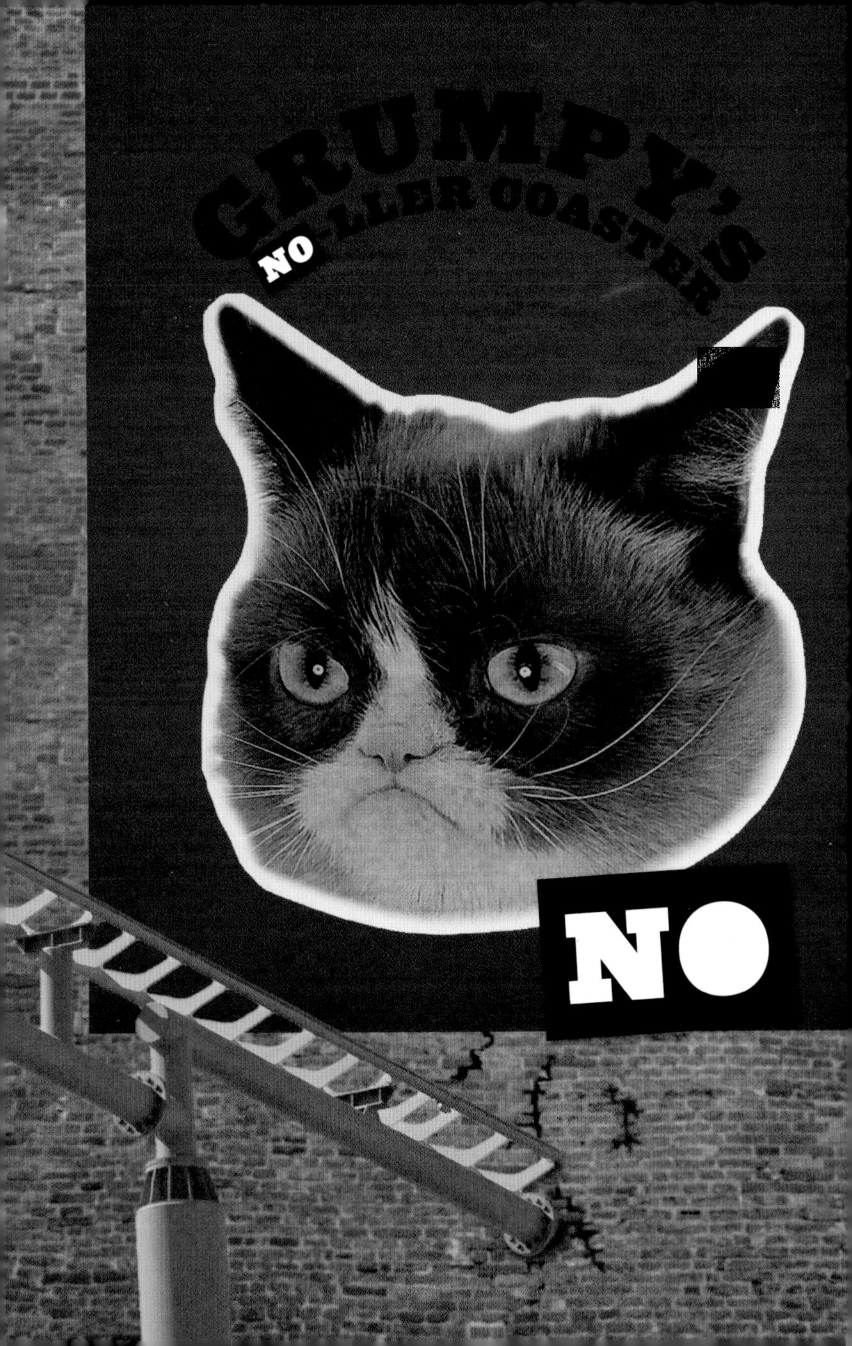
GRUMPY'S
NO-LLER COASTER
NO

Parties

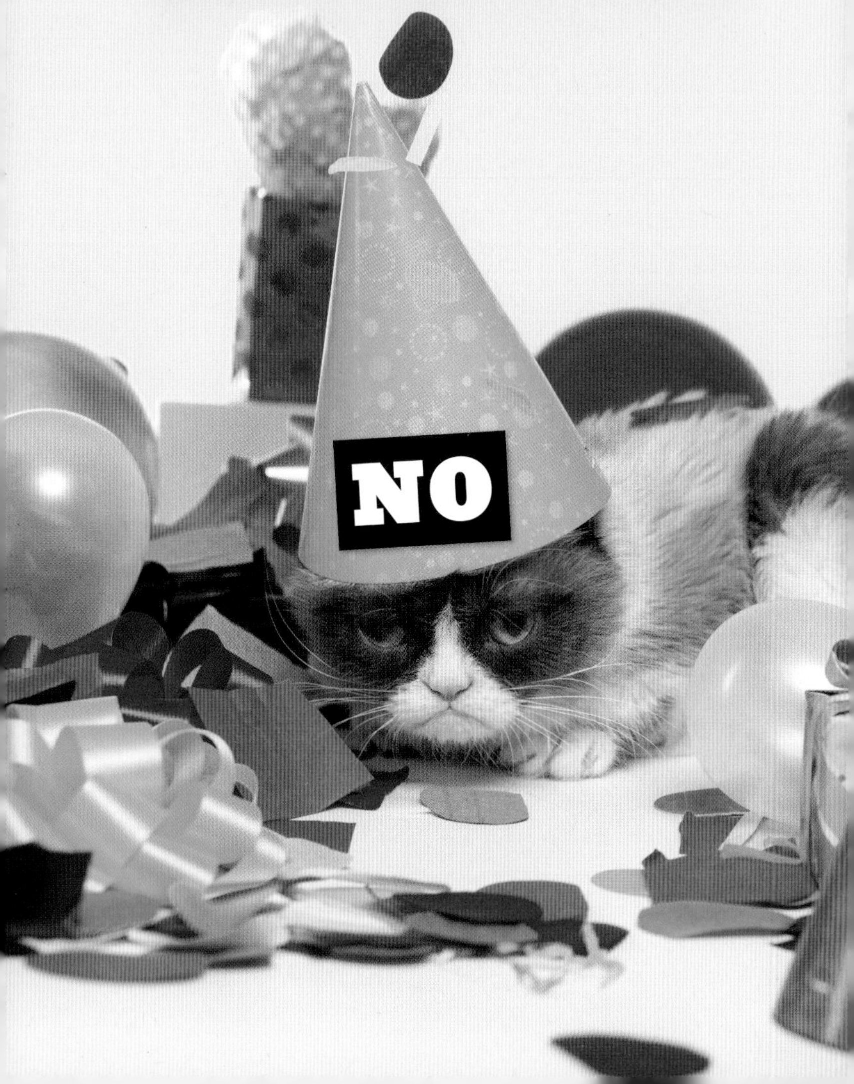
NO

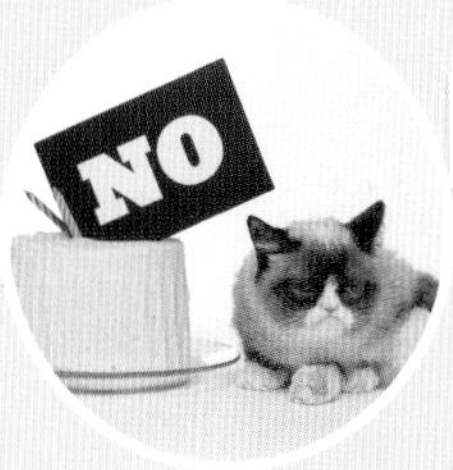
NO

THIS BIRTHDAY IS OFFICIALLY CANCELLED.

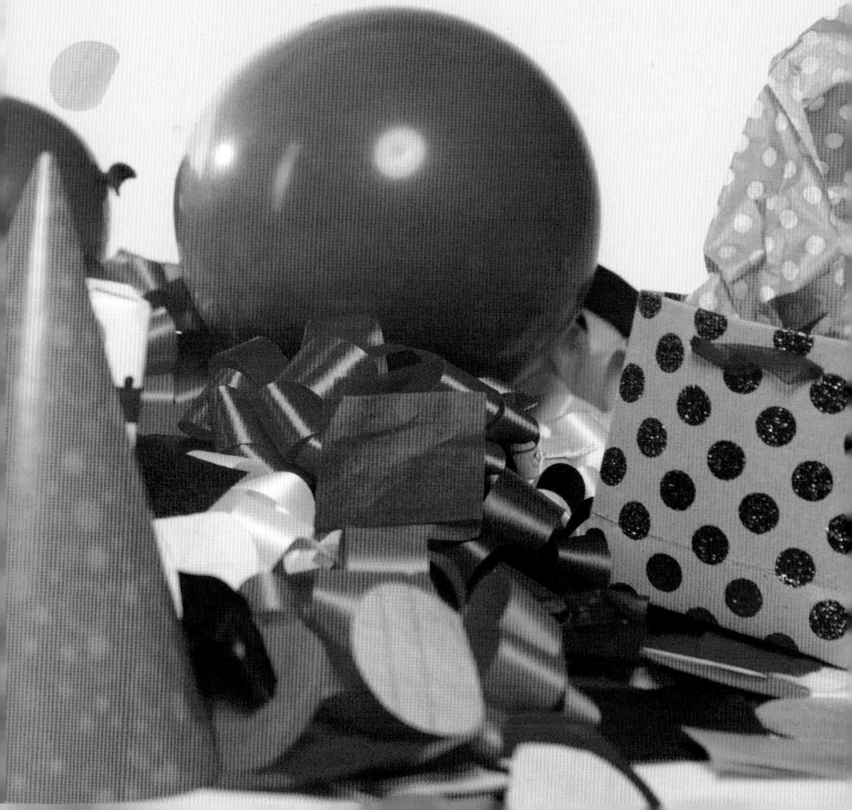

Cuddling

YOU KEEP TRYING.

I KEEP SCRATCHING.

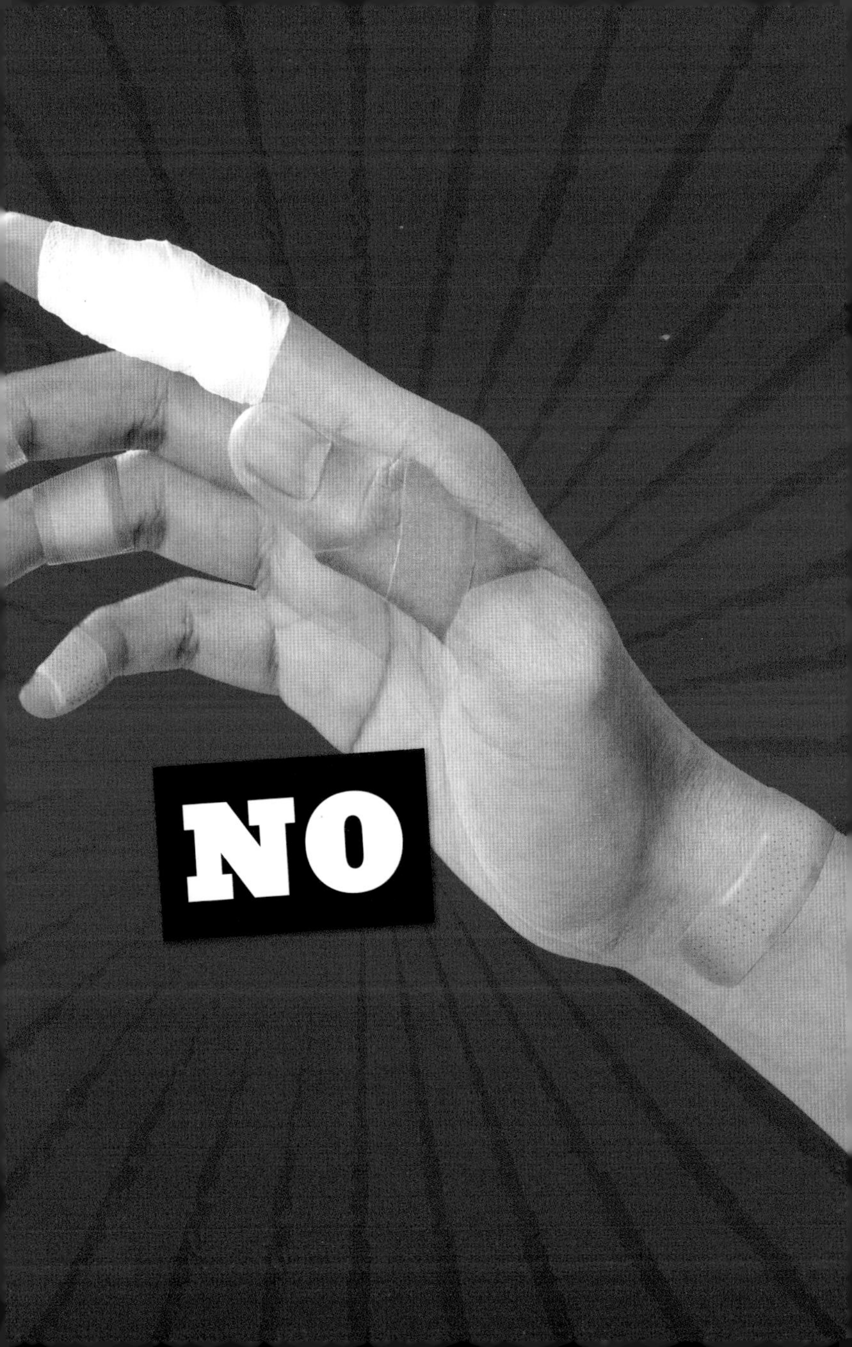
NO

Toys

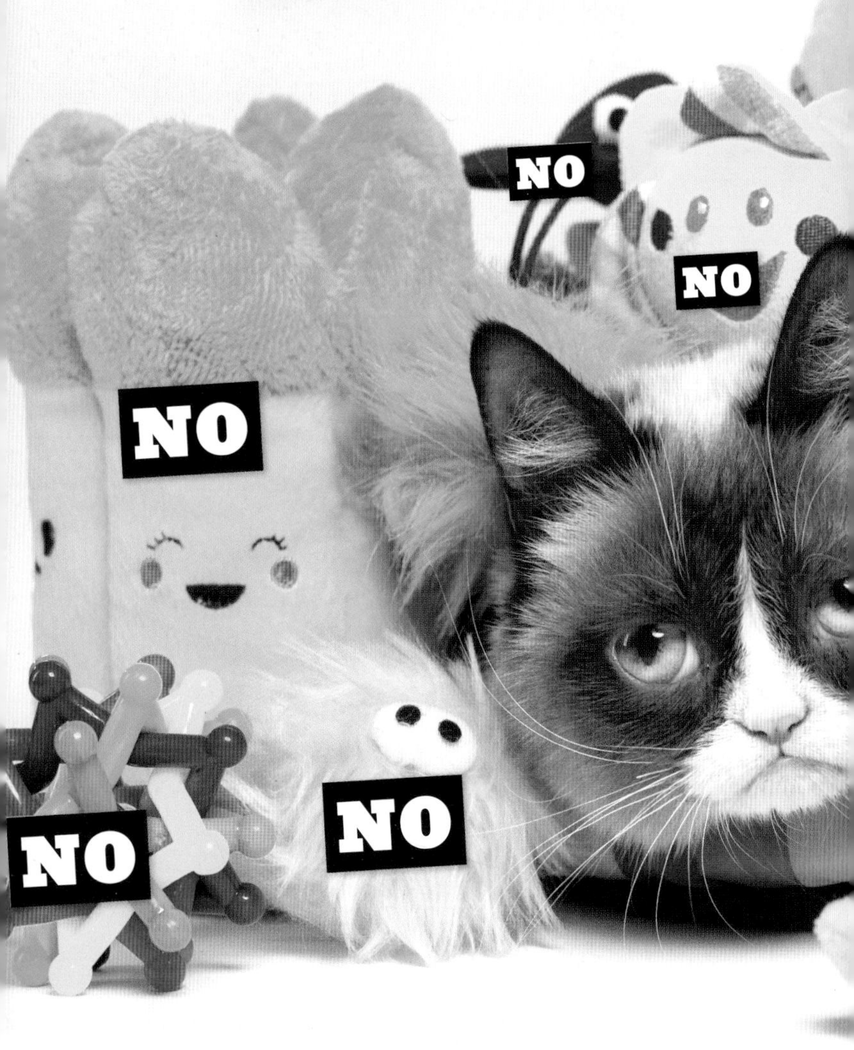
NO
NO
NO
NO
NO

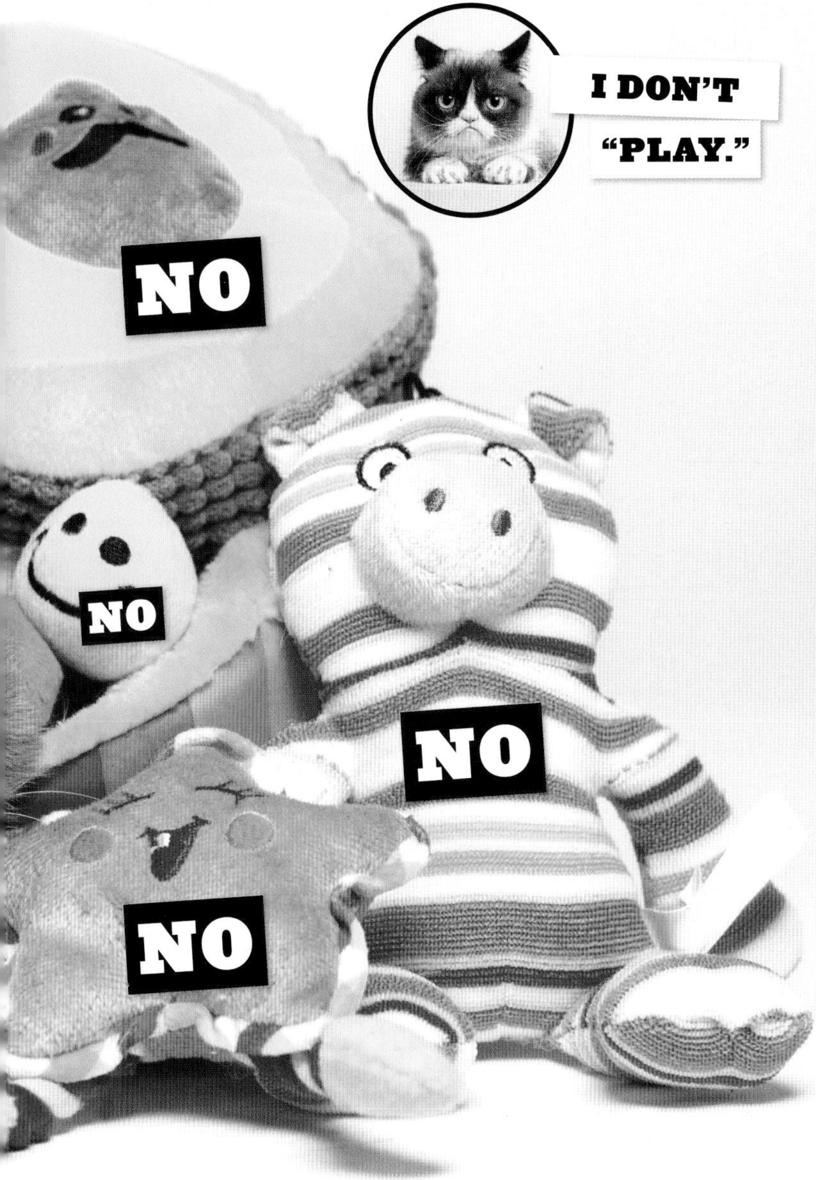
I DON'T
"PLAY."
NO
NO
NO
NO

Days of the Week

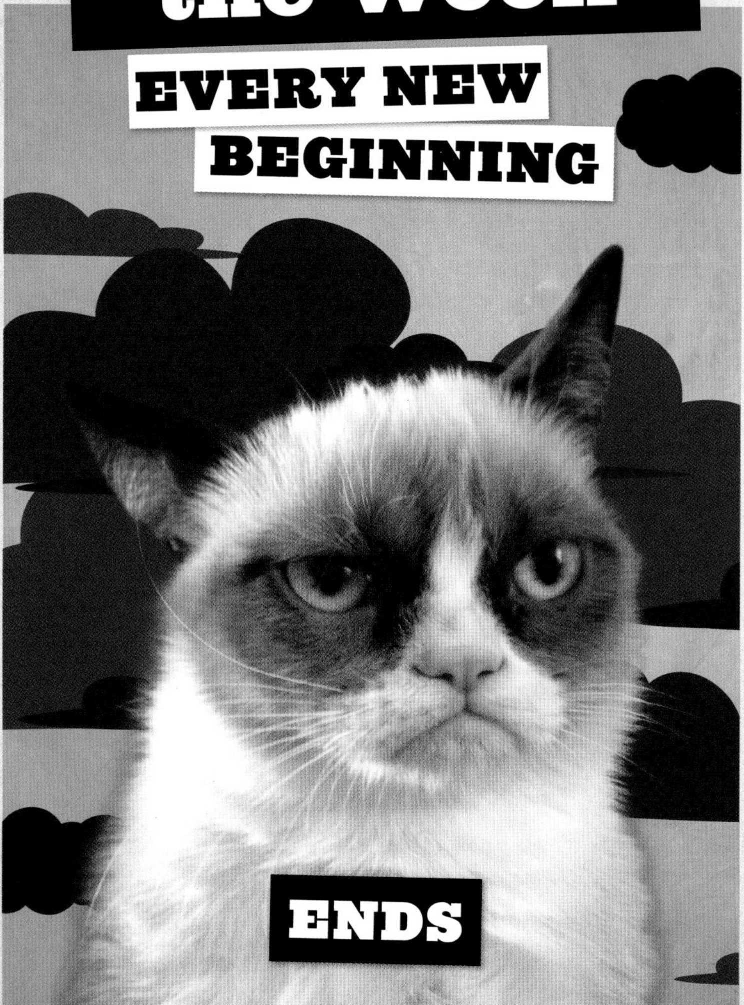
EVERY NEW BEGINNING
ENDS

SUNDAY

NO

SPORTS ARE ON, PROBABLY. I JUST REMIND MYSELF THAT HALF THE TEAMS LOSE.

MONDAY

OKAY, ACTUALLY.

EVERYONE IS MISERABLE. GOAL: MAKE EVERY DAY A MONDAY.

TUESDAY

NO

NOT MONDAY.

WEDNESDAY

NO

EVEN FURTHER FROM MONDAY.

THURSDAY

NO

ALMOST FRIDAY. PEOPLE SEEM ... HOPEFUL? UGH.

FRIDAY

NO

THE WORST.

SATURDAY

NO

I REFUSE TO OPEN MY EYES ON THIS DAY BUT I ASSUME IT'S TERRIBLE, TOO.

Swimming

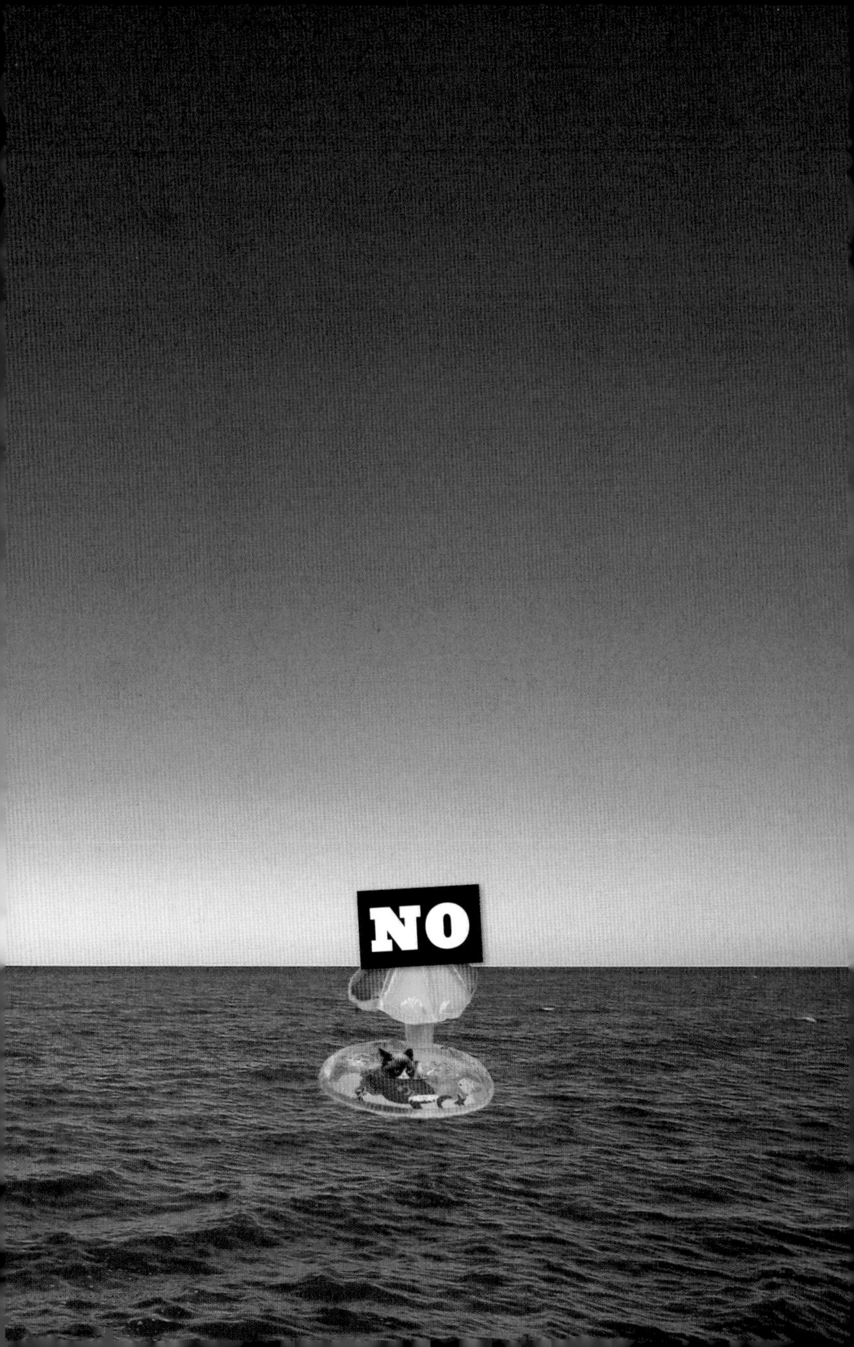
NO

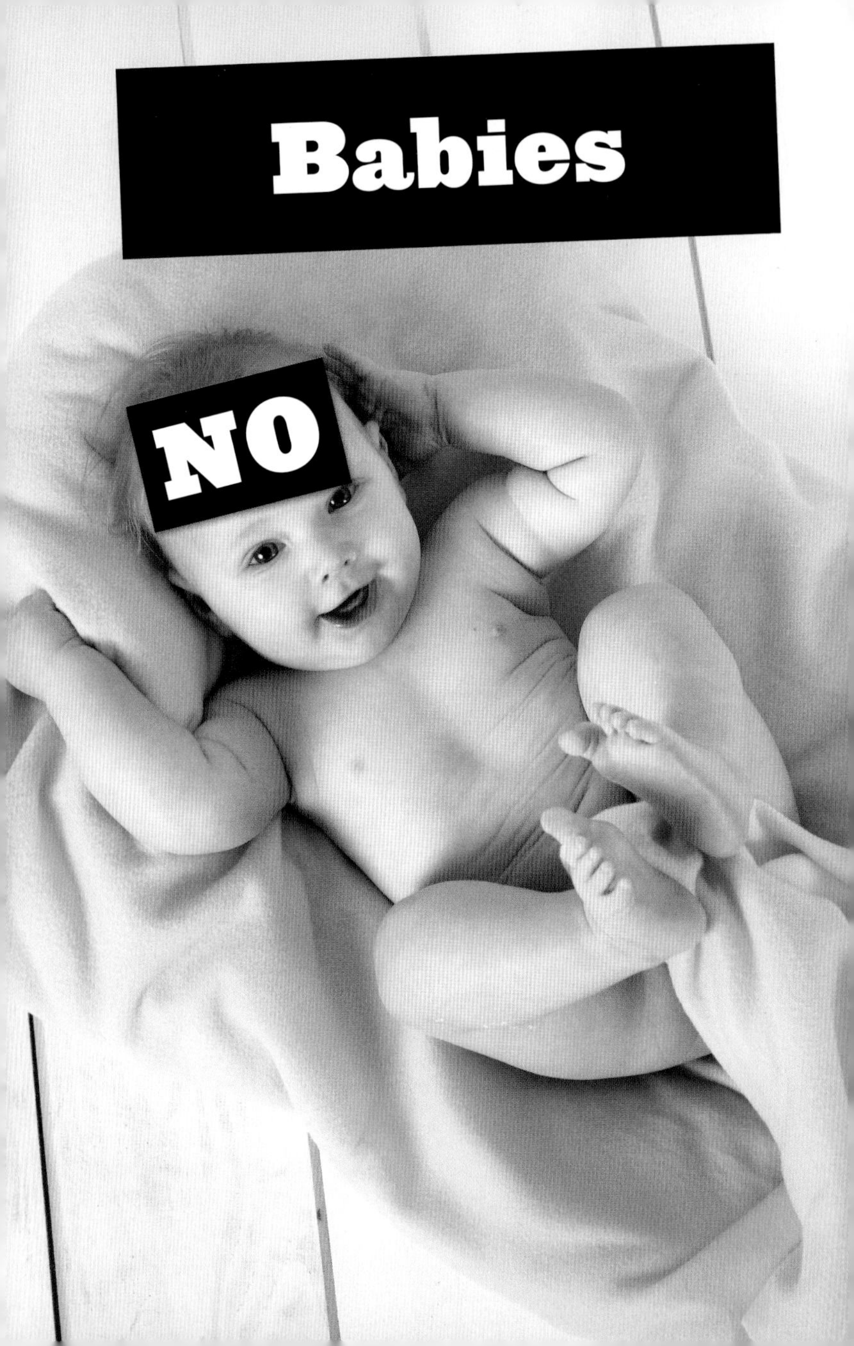
Babies
NO

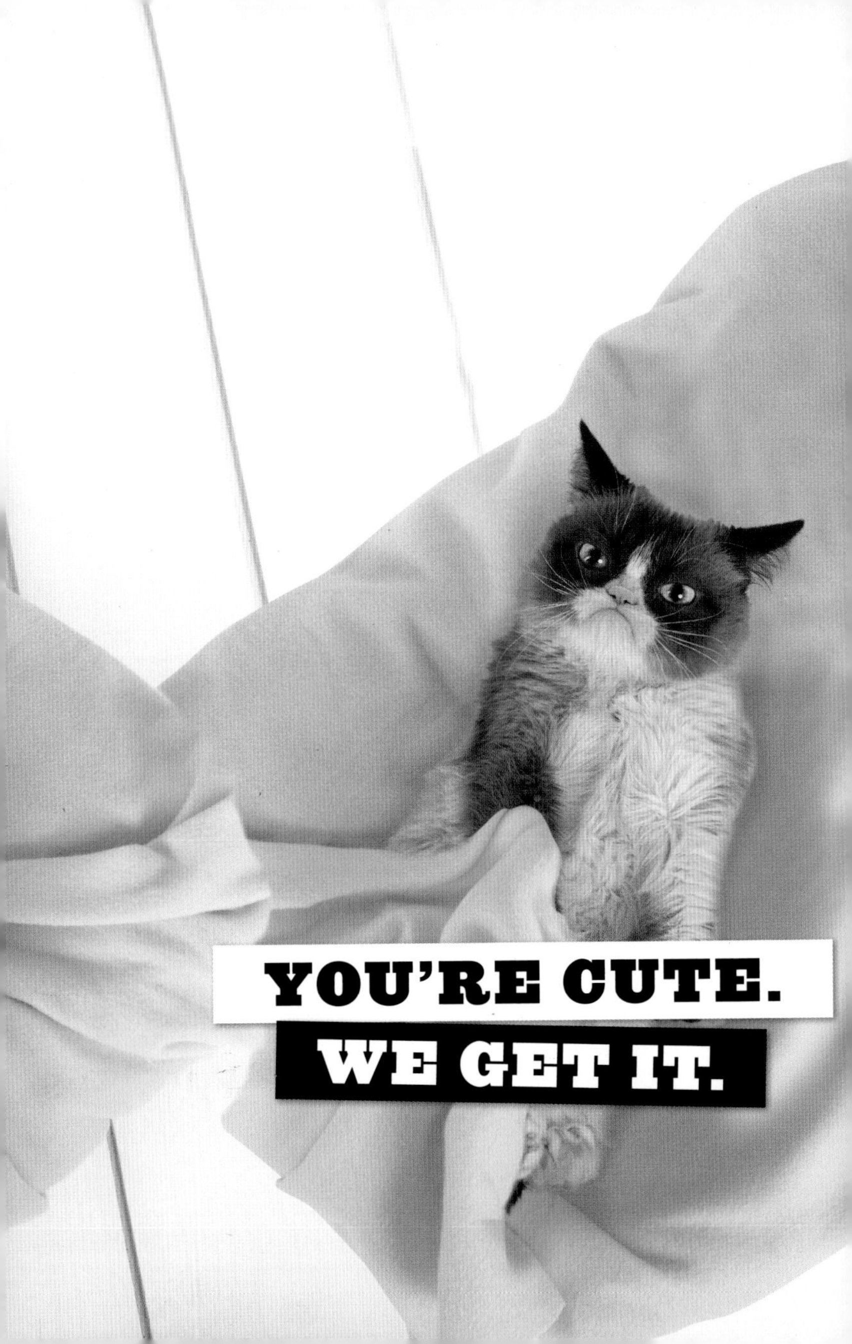
YOU'RE CUTE.
WE GET IT.

News

Grumpy

ISSUE: WHATEVER

WHY DON'T YOU JU

NOTHING IMPOR

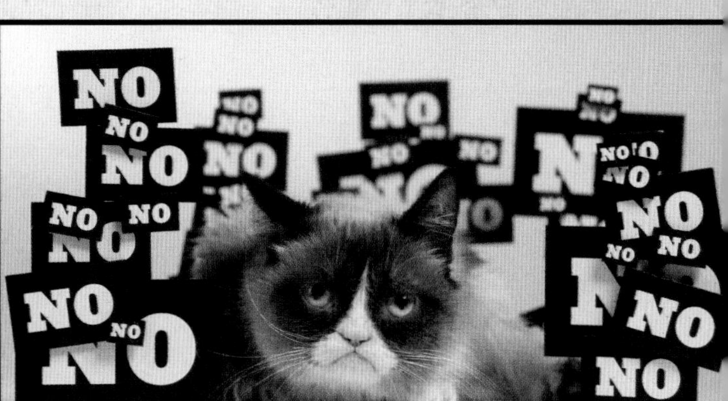
NO
NO
NO
NO
NO
NO
NO
NO
NO
NO
NO
NO
NO
NO
NO
NO
NO

Grumpy Cat is on a mission to "NO" everything.

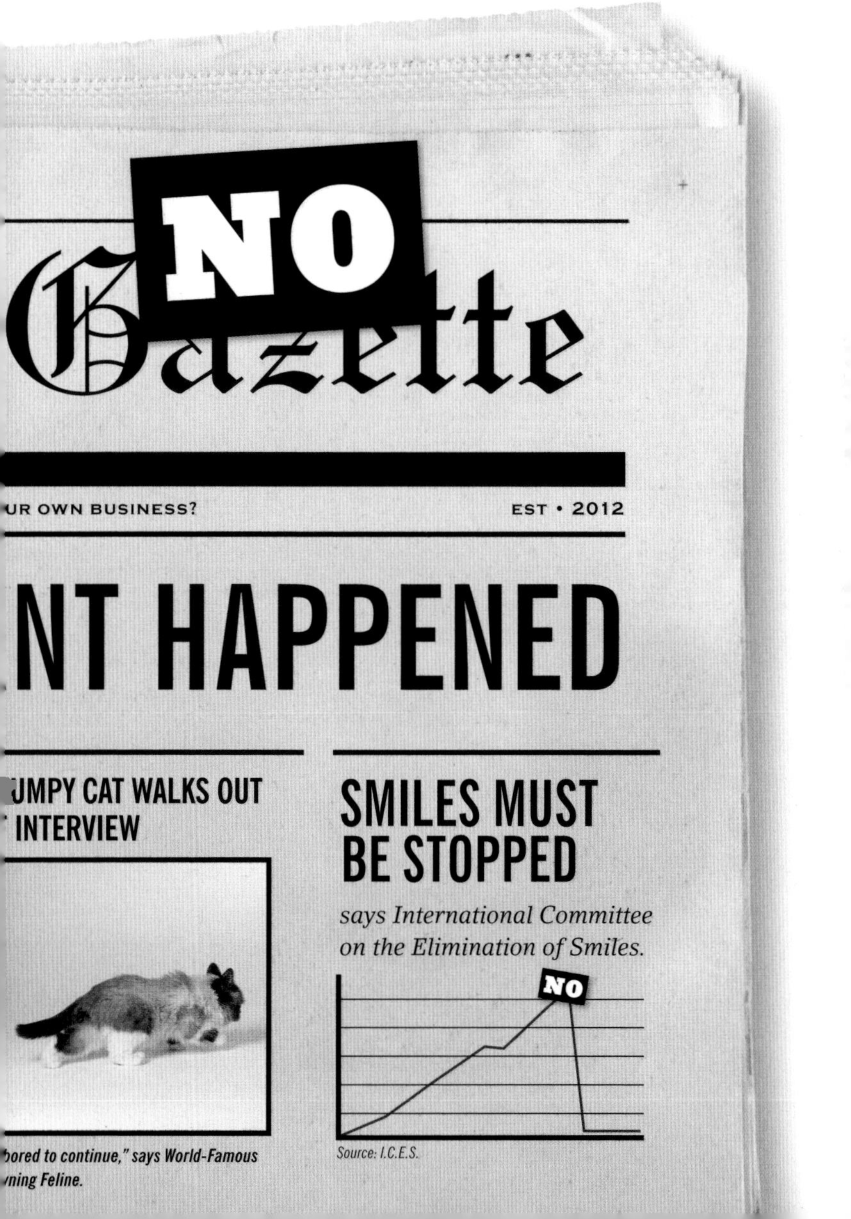

NO
Gazette

UR OWN BUSINESS?

EST • 2012

NT HAPPENED

UMPY CAT WALKS OUT
INTERVIEW

bored to continue," says World-Famous
ning Feline.

SMILES MUST
BE STOPPED

says International Committee on the Elimination of Smiles.

NO

Source: I.C.E.S.

Movies

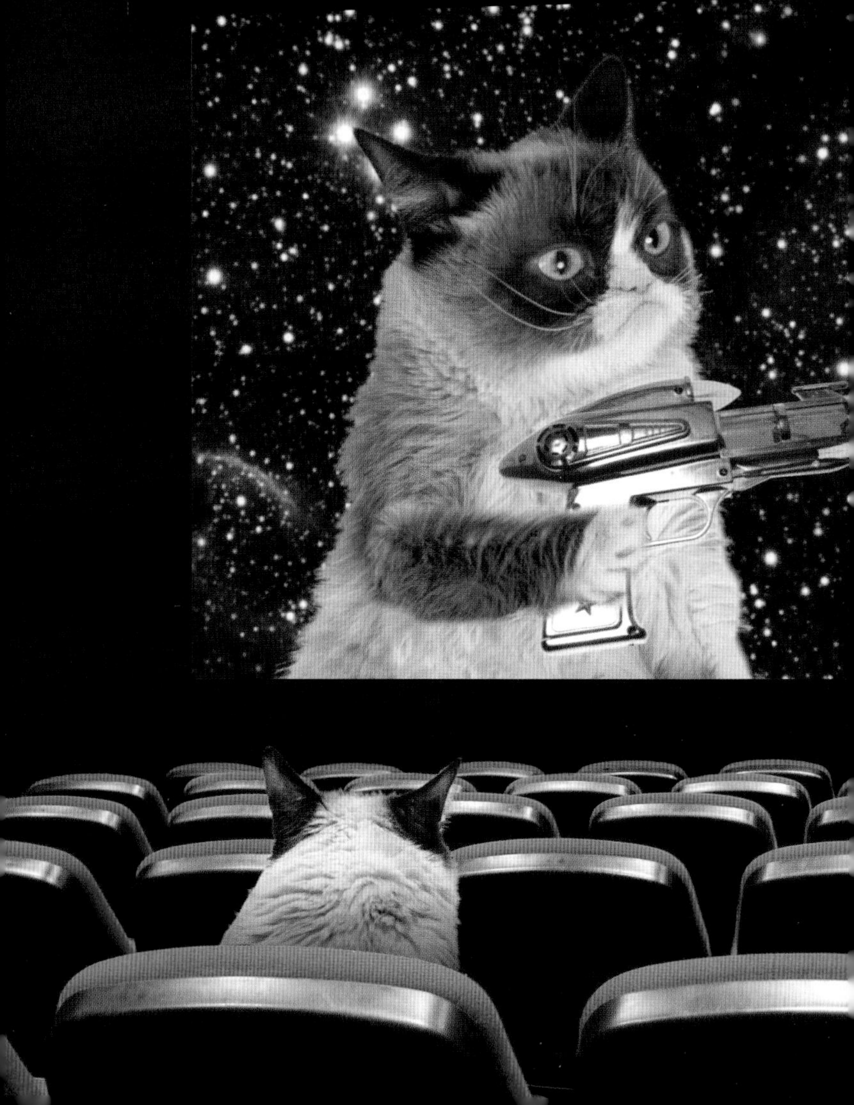

The
from
NO

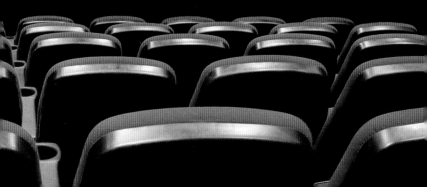

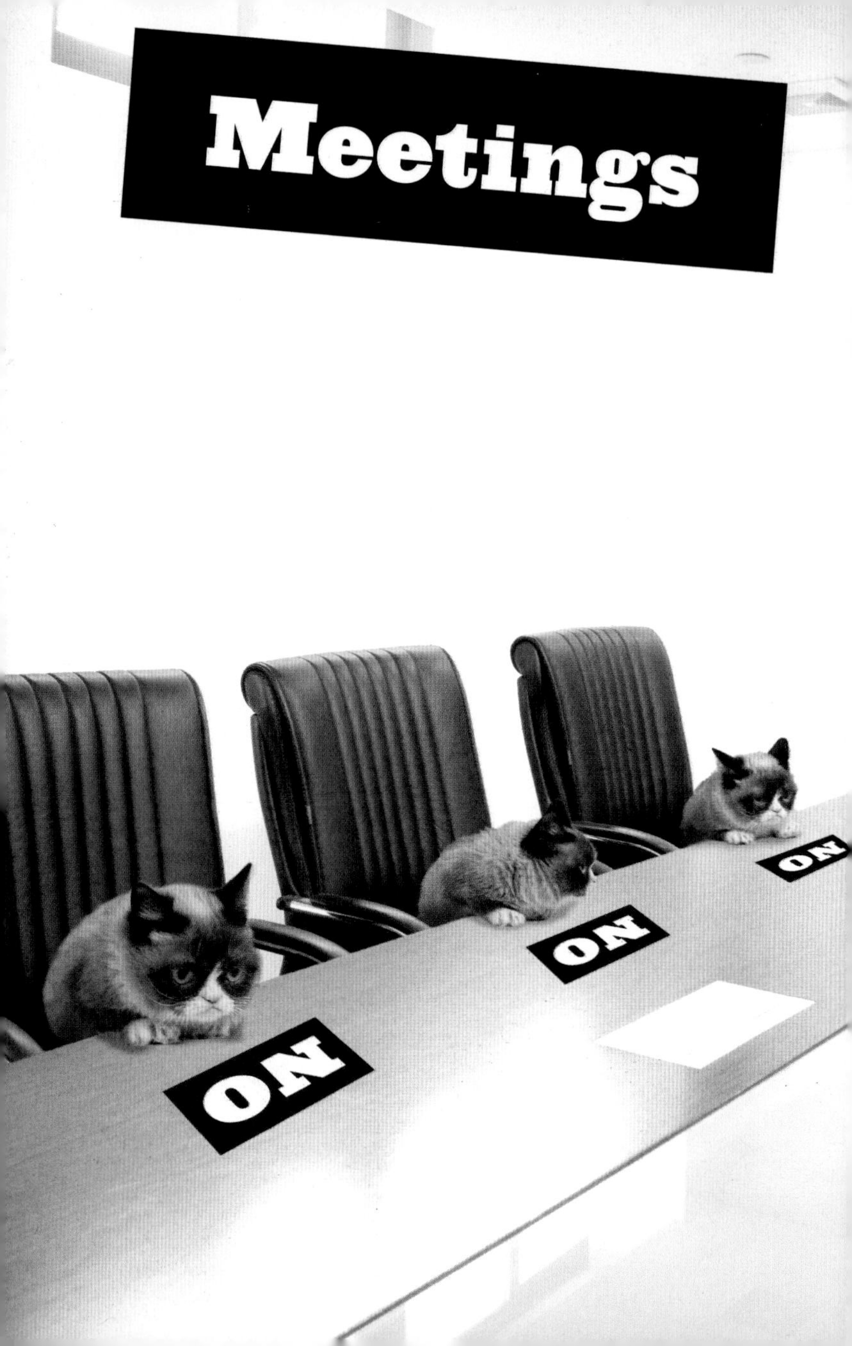
Meetings
NO
NO
NO

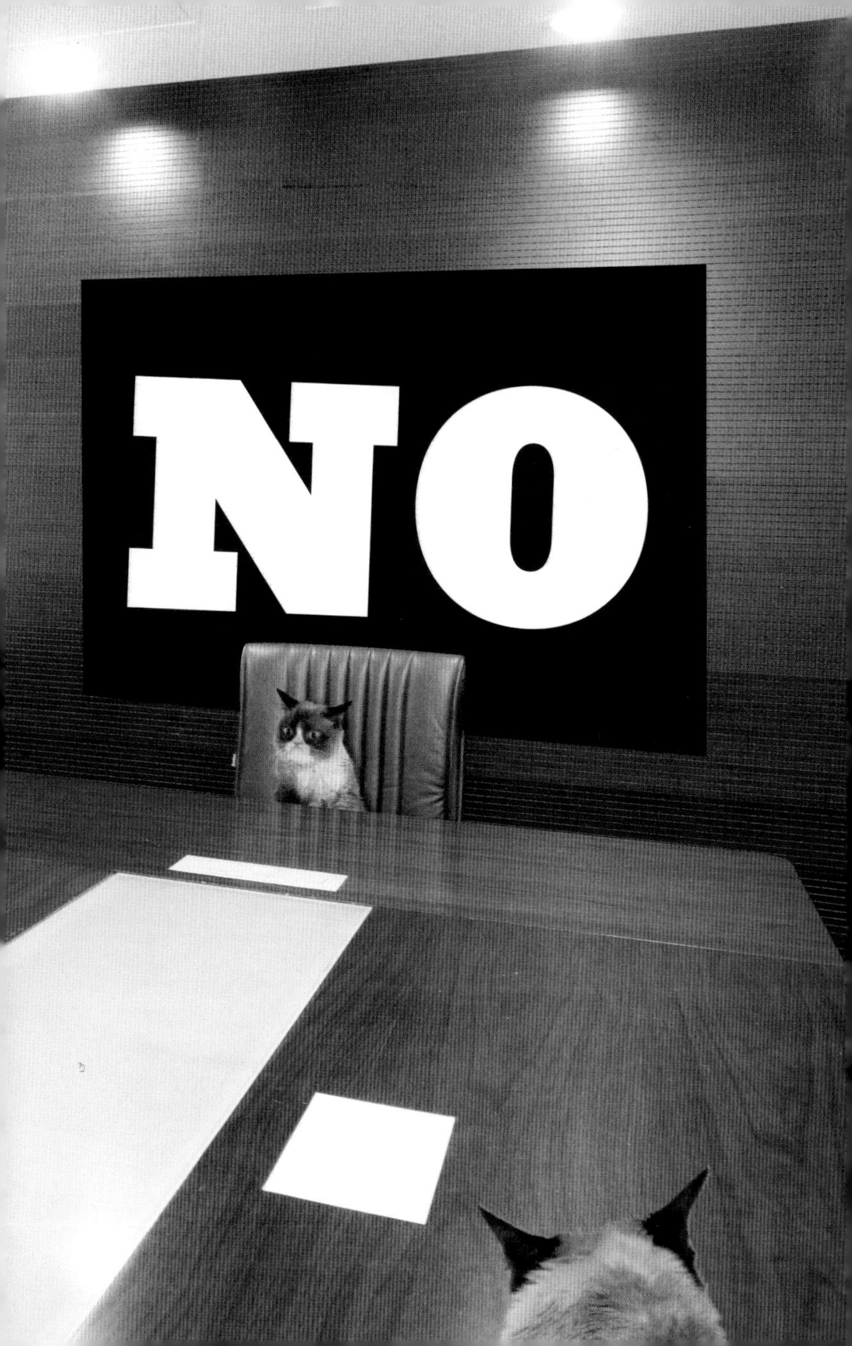
NO

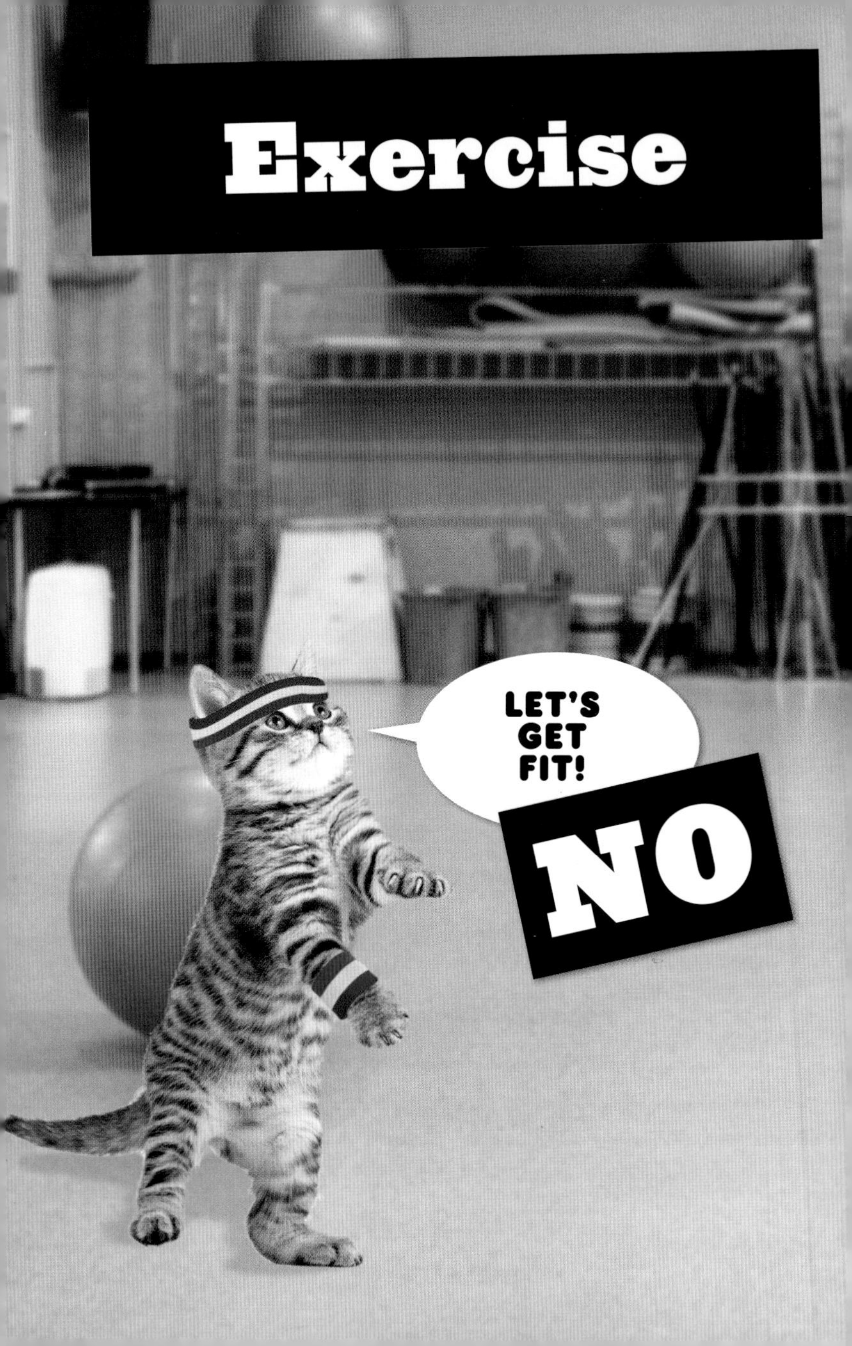
Exercise
LET'S GET FIT!
NO

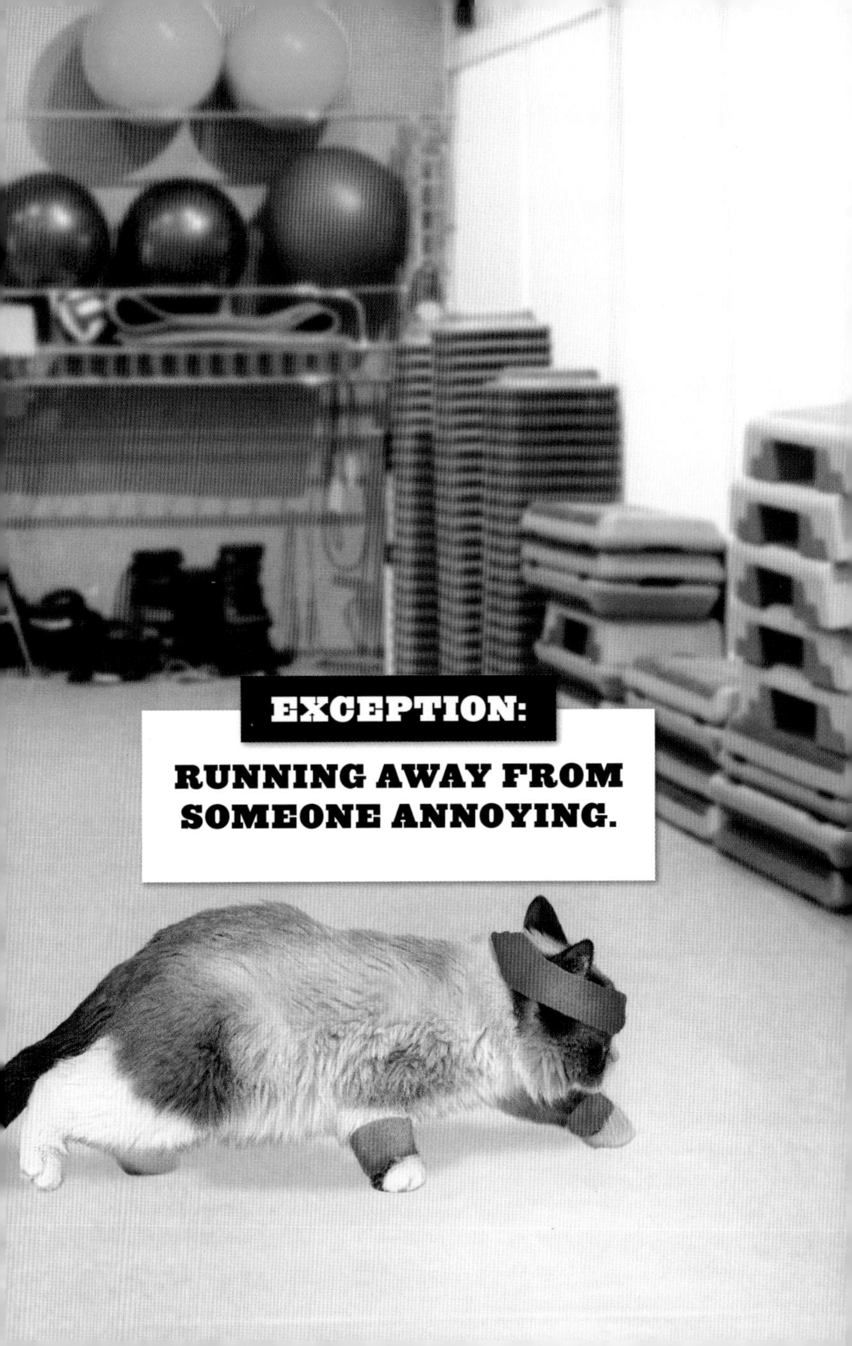
EXCEPTION:
RUNNING AWAY FROM SOMEONE ANNOYING.

Presents

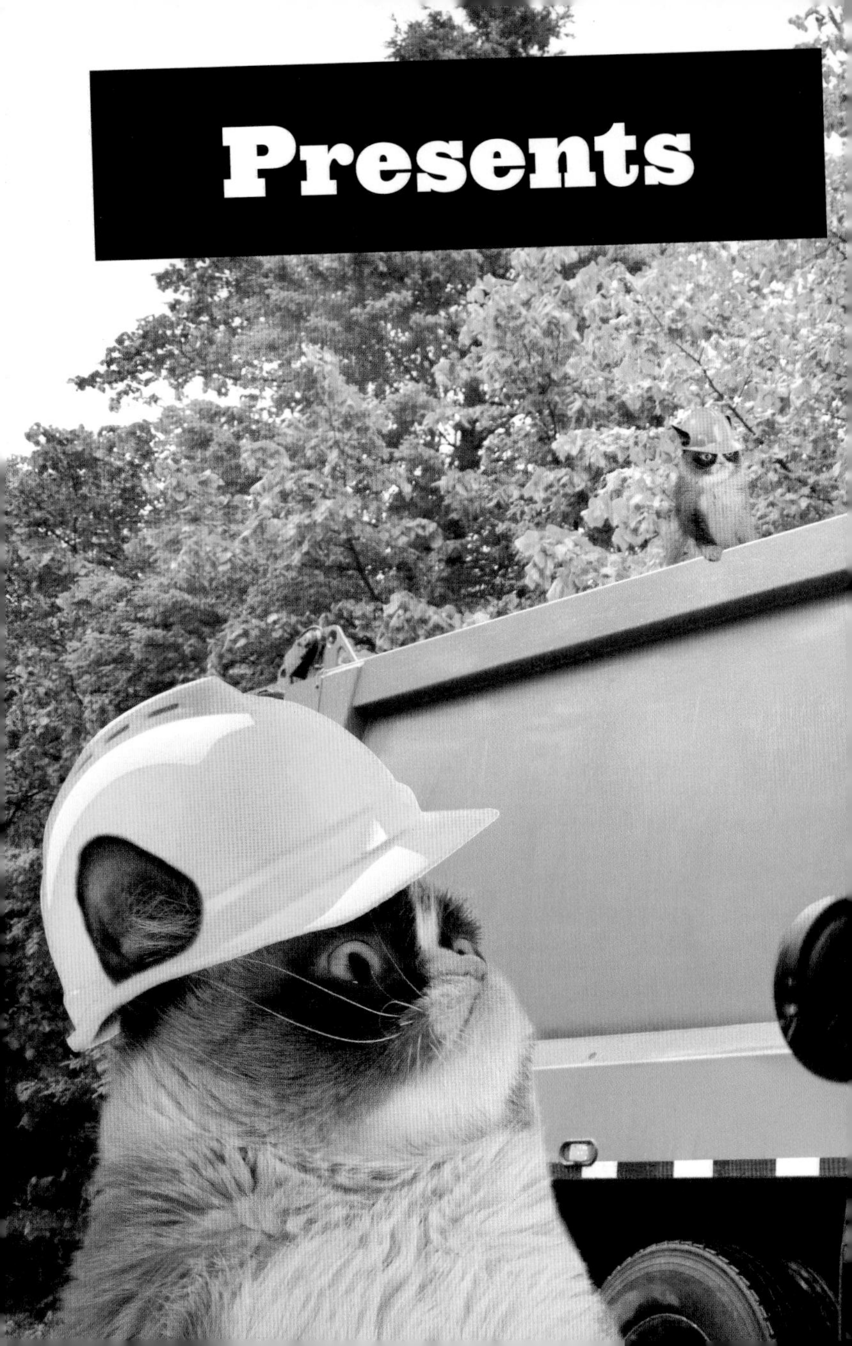

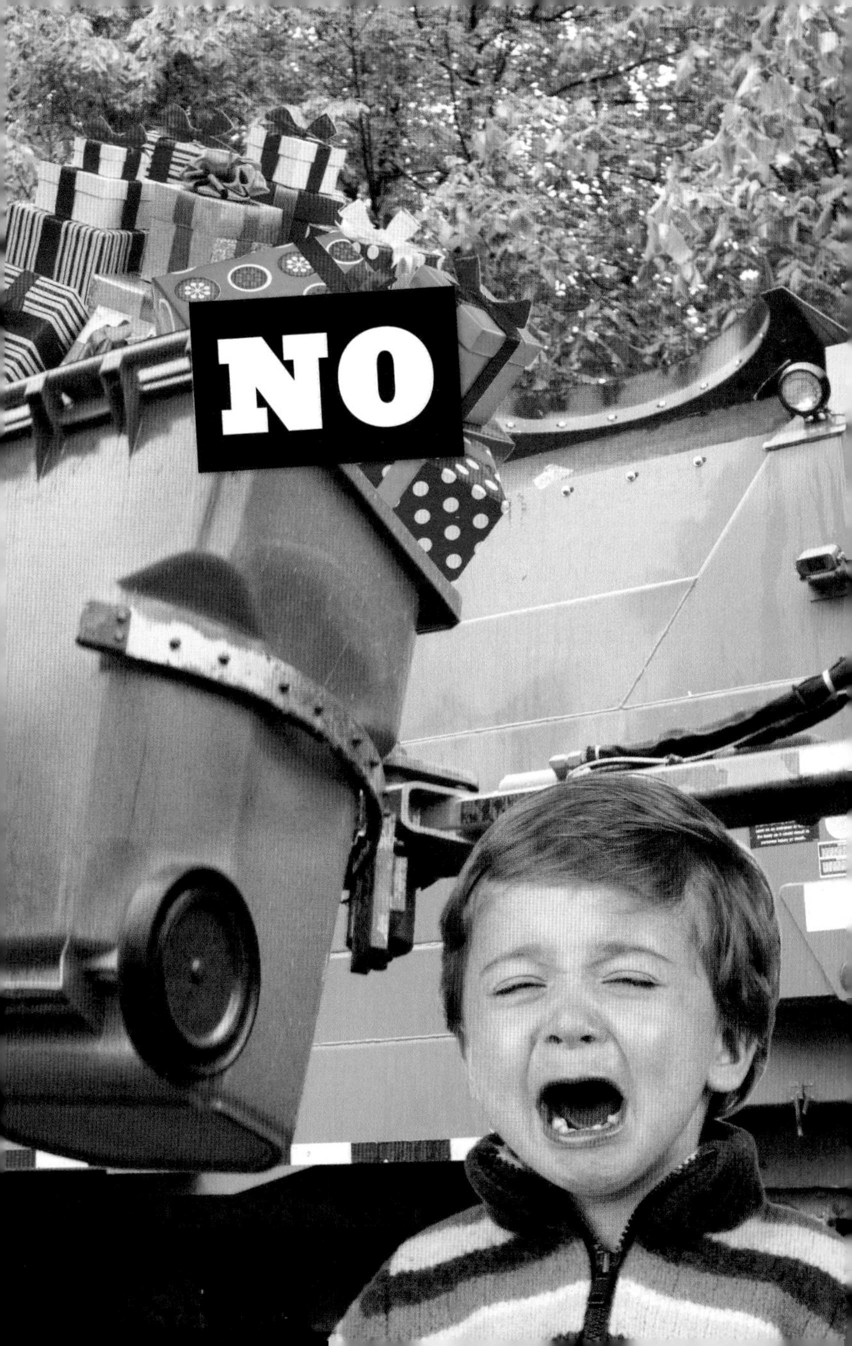
NO

Driving

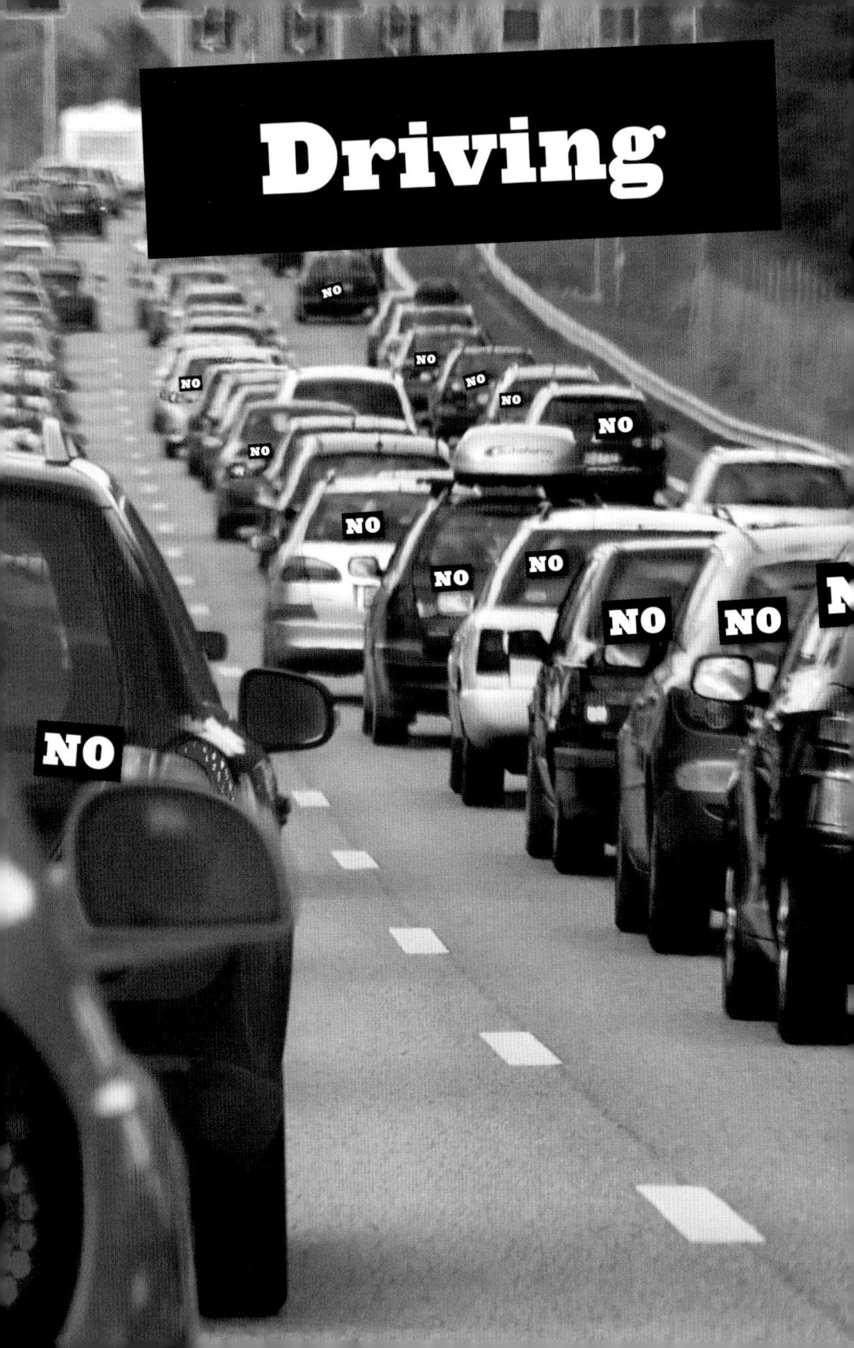
NO
NO
NO
NO
NO
NO
NO
NO
NO
NO
NO
NO
NO
NO

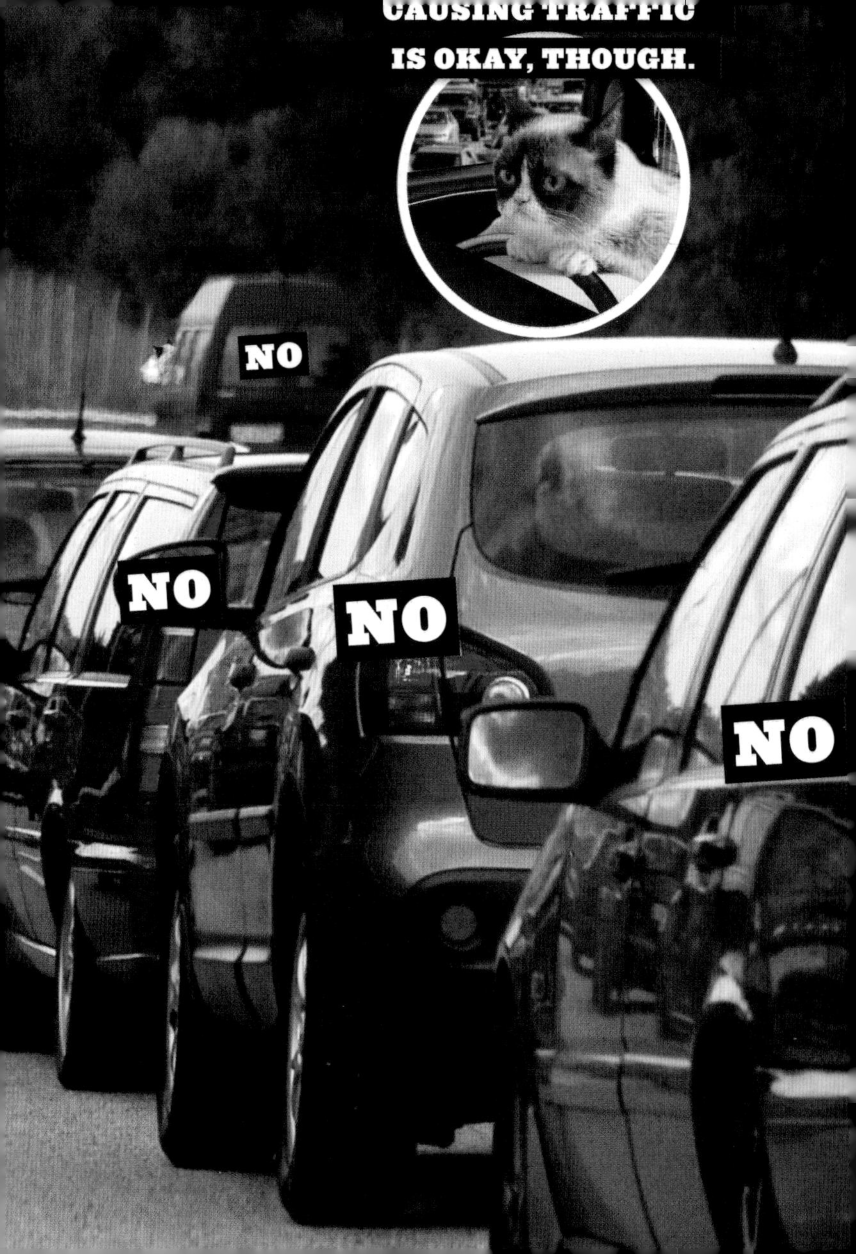
CAUSING TRAFFIC
IS OKAY, THOUGH.
NO
NO
NO
NO

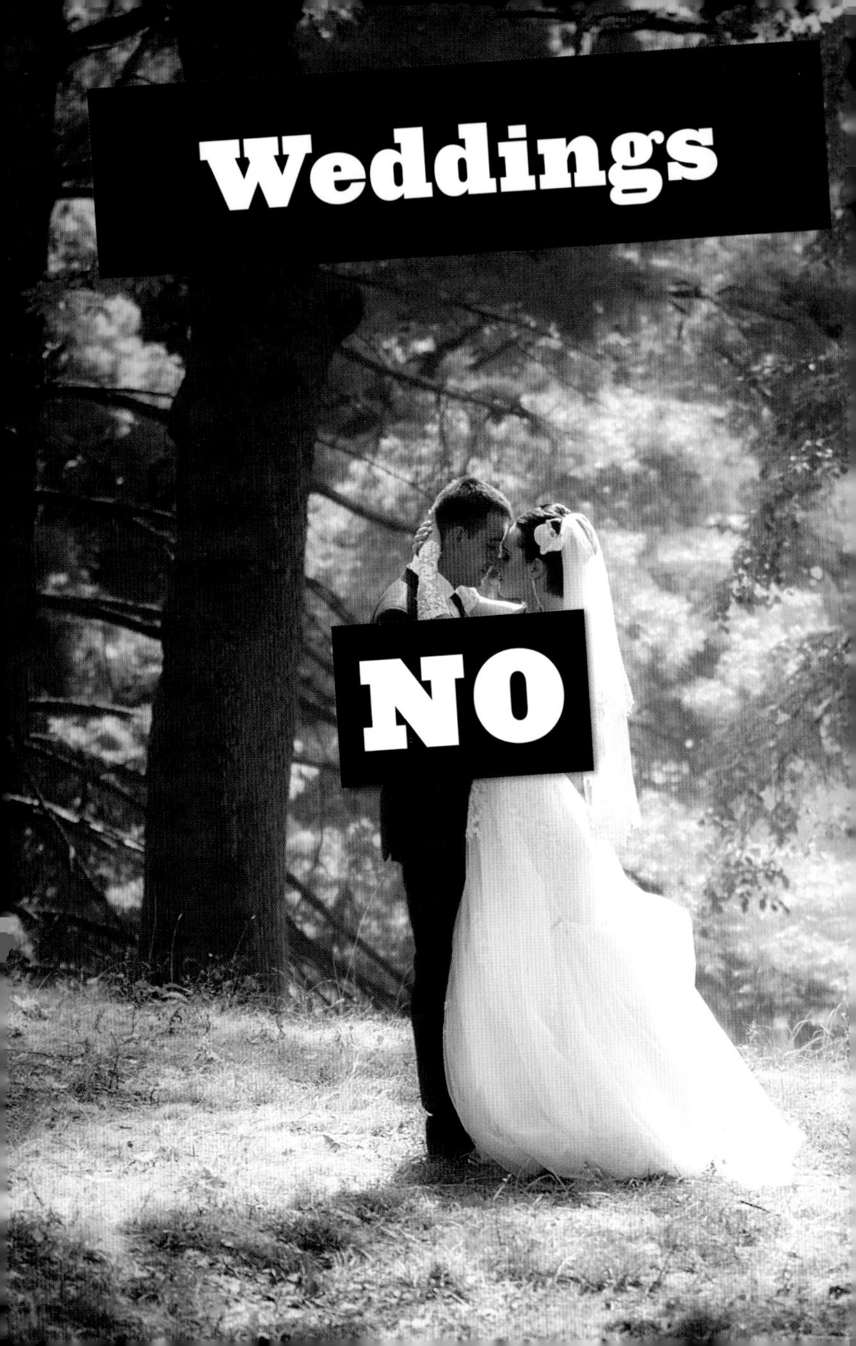
Weddings
NO

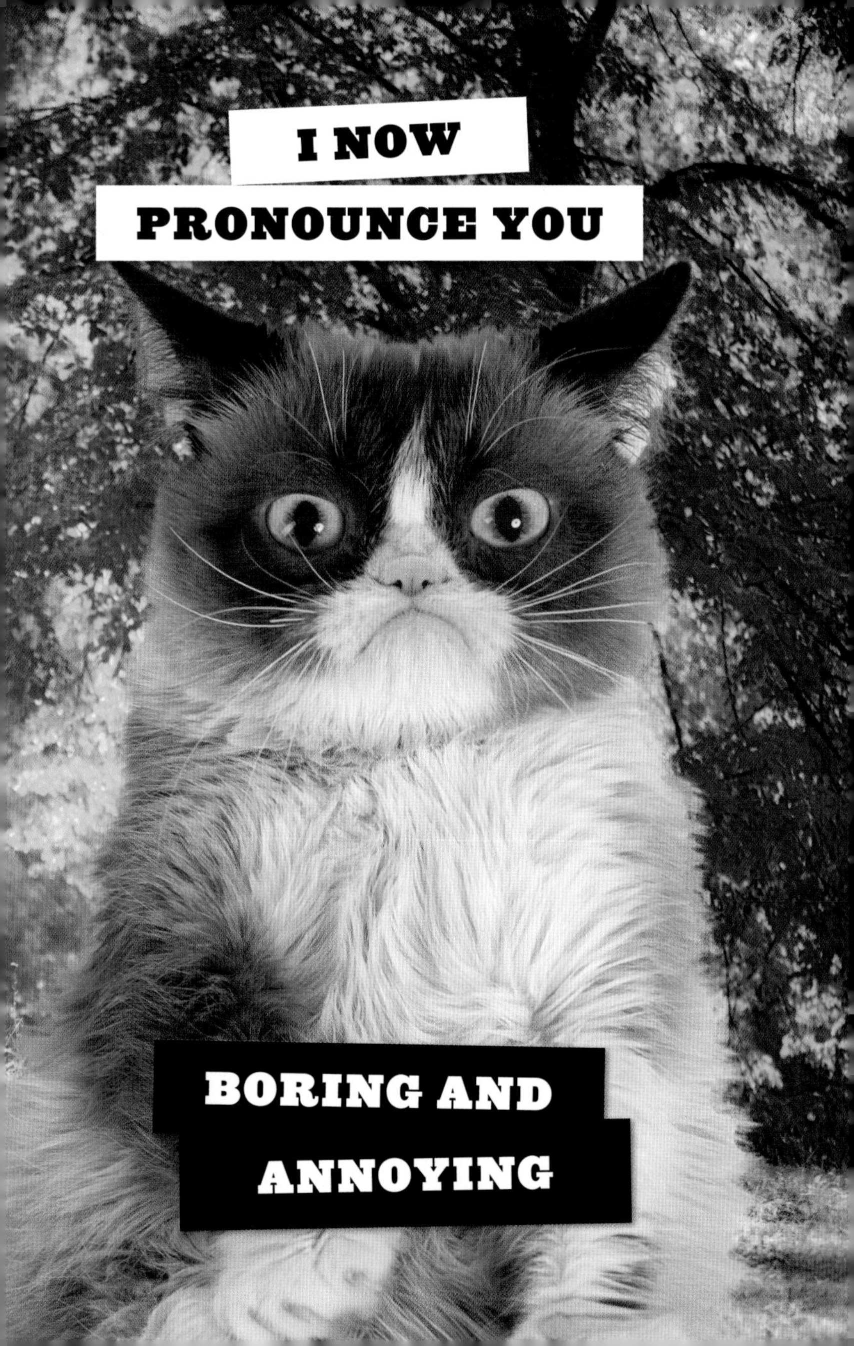
I NOW
PRONOUNCE YOU
BORING AND
ANNOYING

Texting

NO

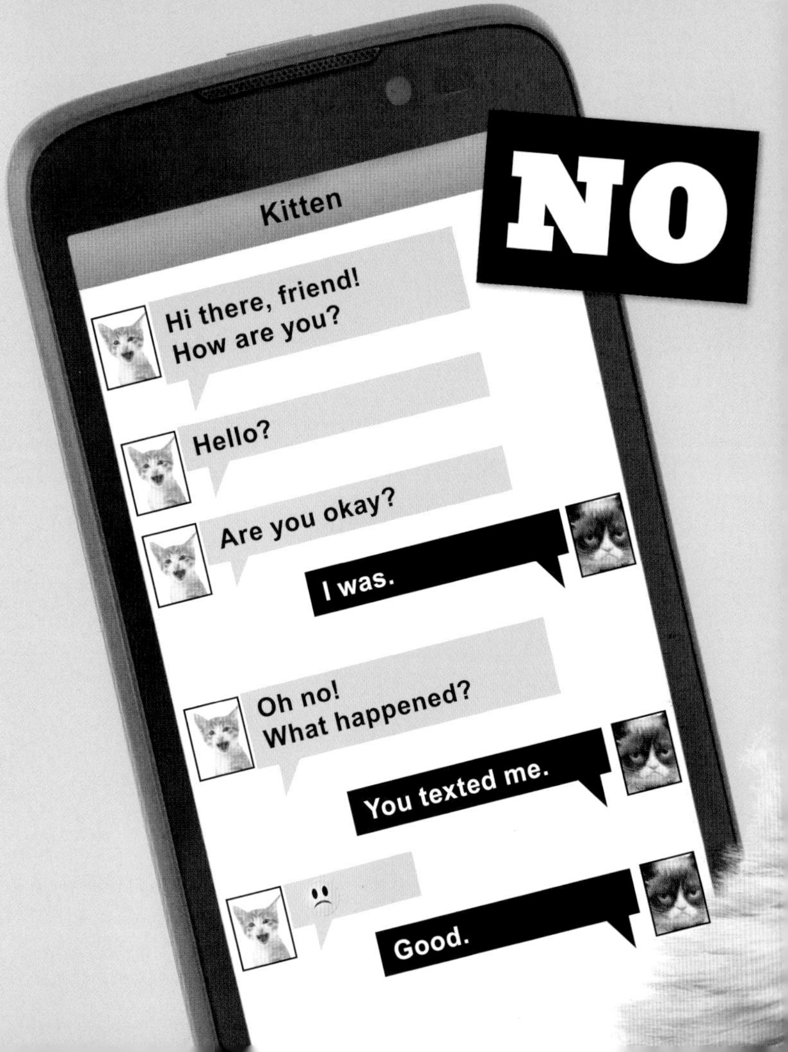

Kitten
Hi there, friend!
How are you?
Hello?
Are you okay?
I was.
Oh no!
What happened?
You texted me.
Good.

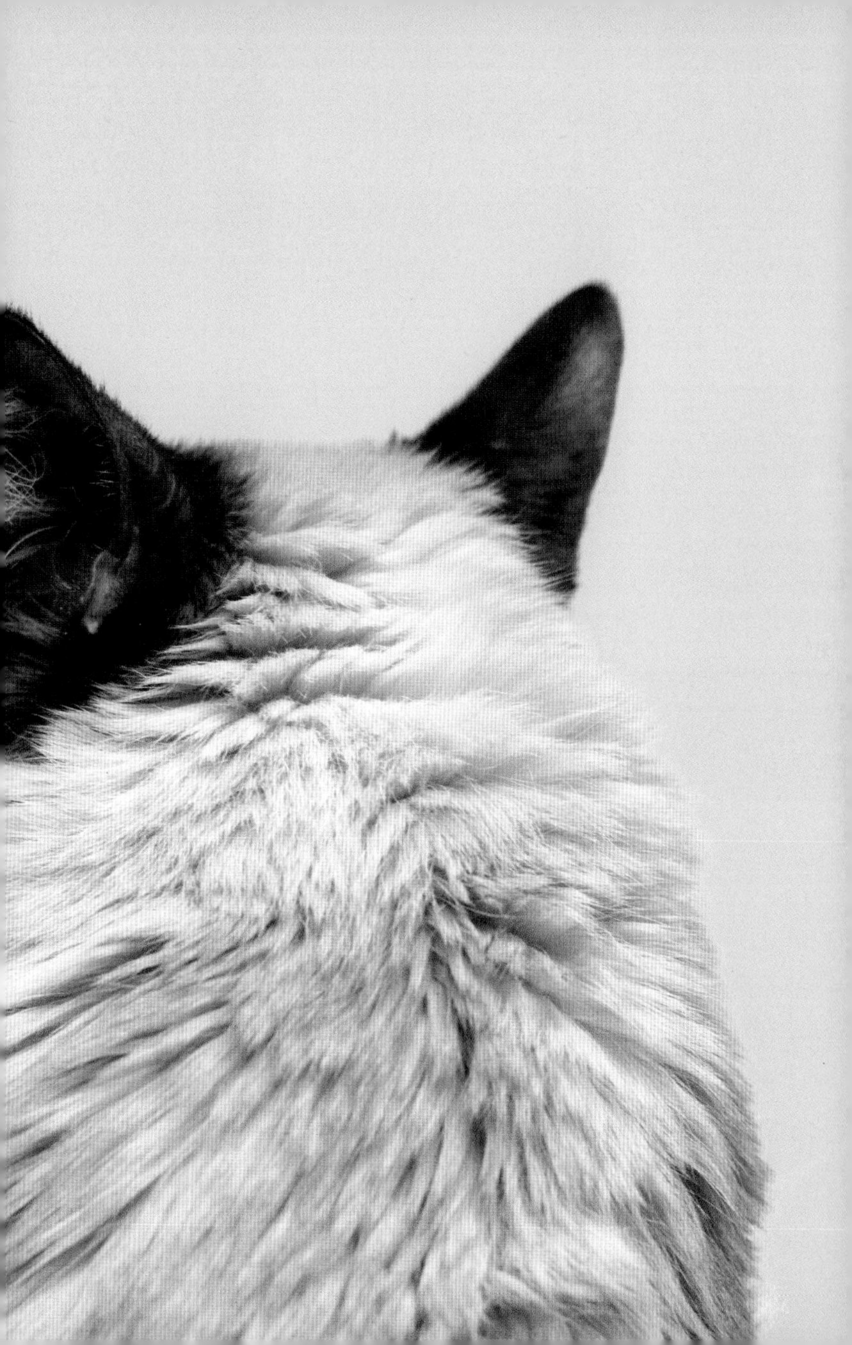

Fashion

THEN

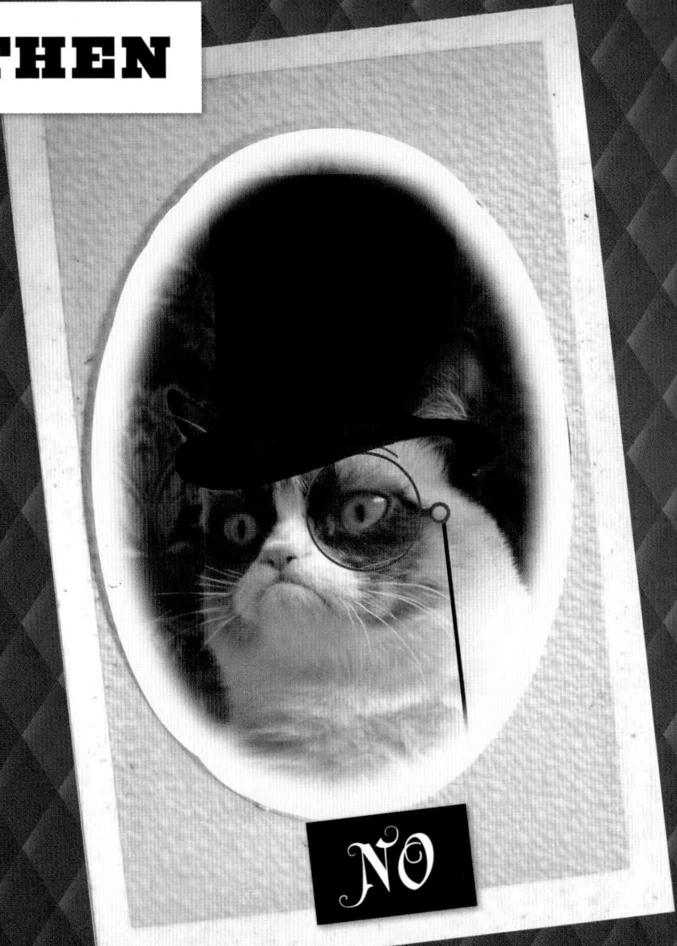
NO

NOW

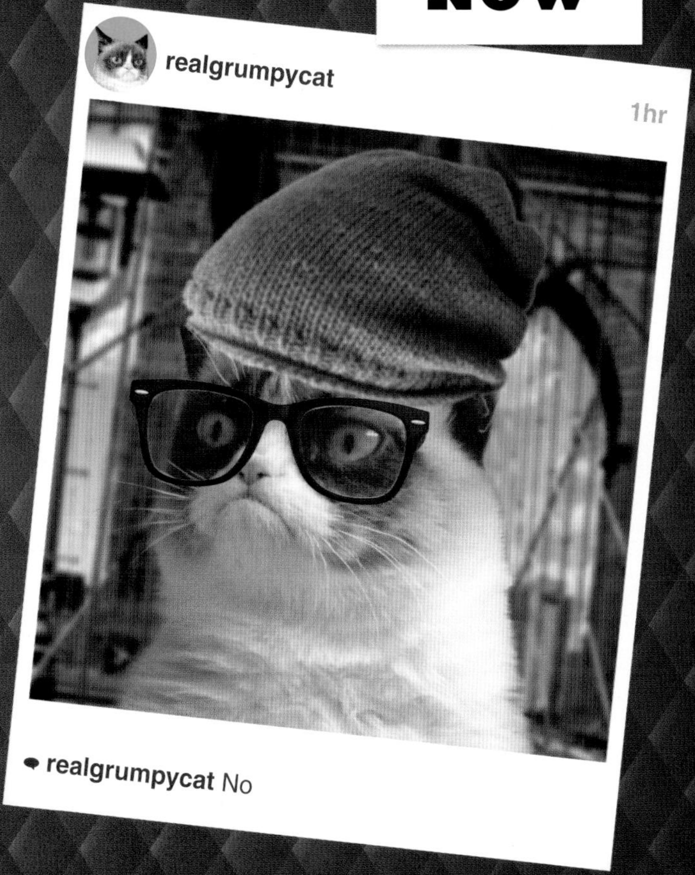
realgrumpycat
1hr
realgrumpycat No

History

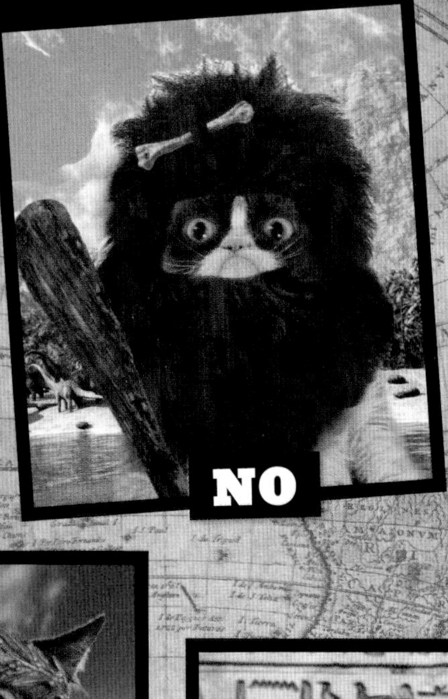
NO

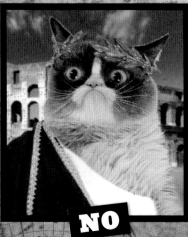

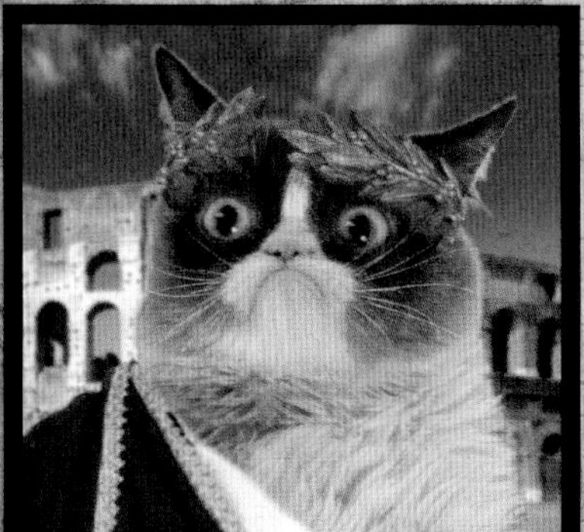
NO

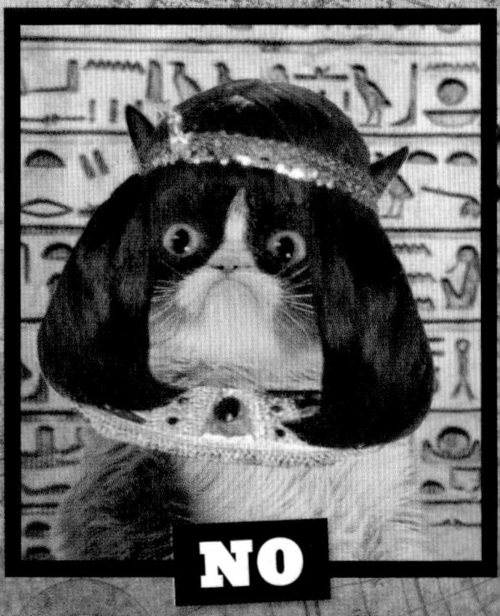
NO

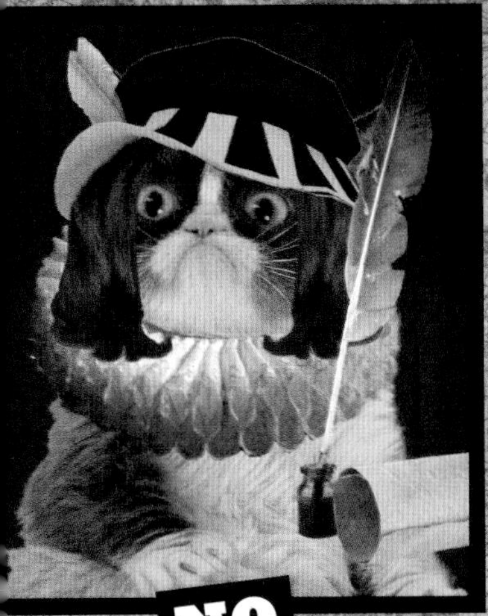

NO

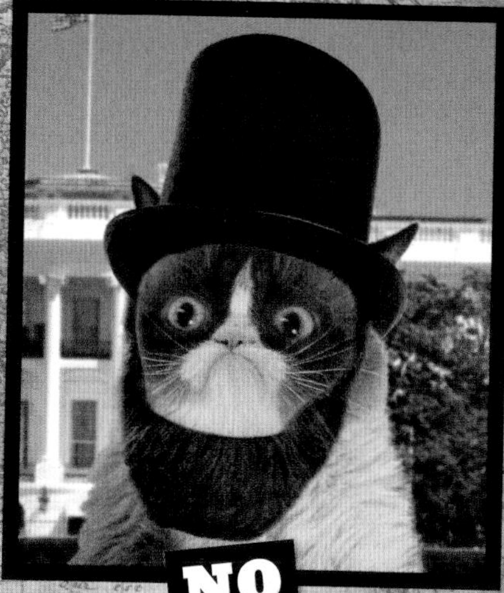

NO

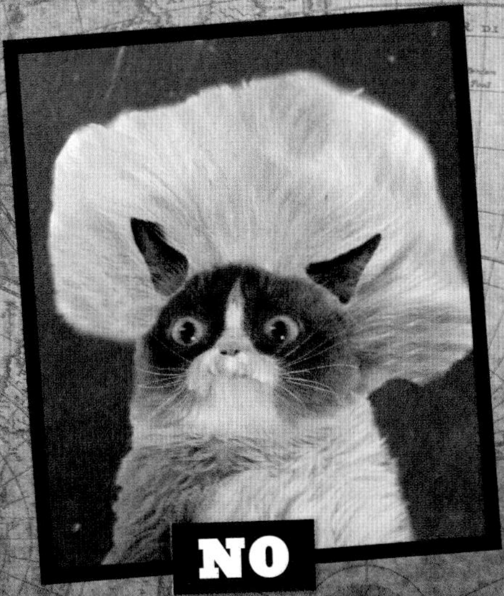

NO

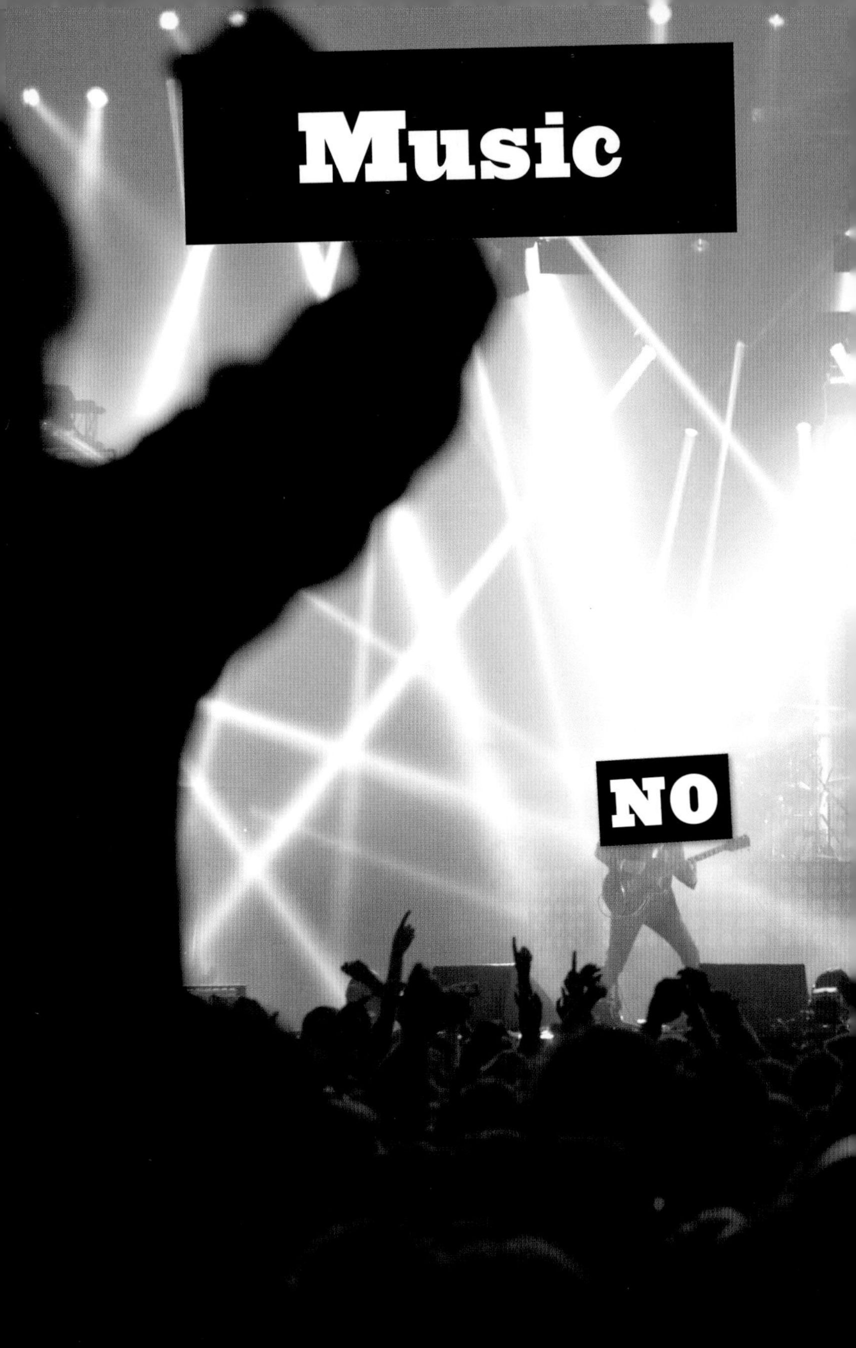
Music
NO

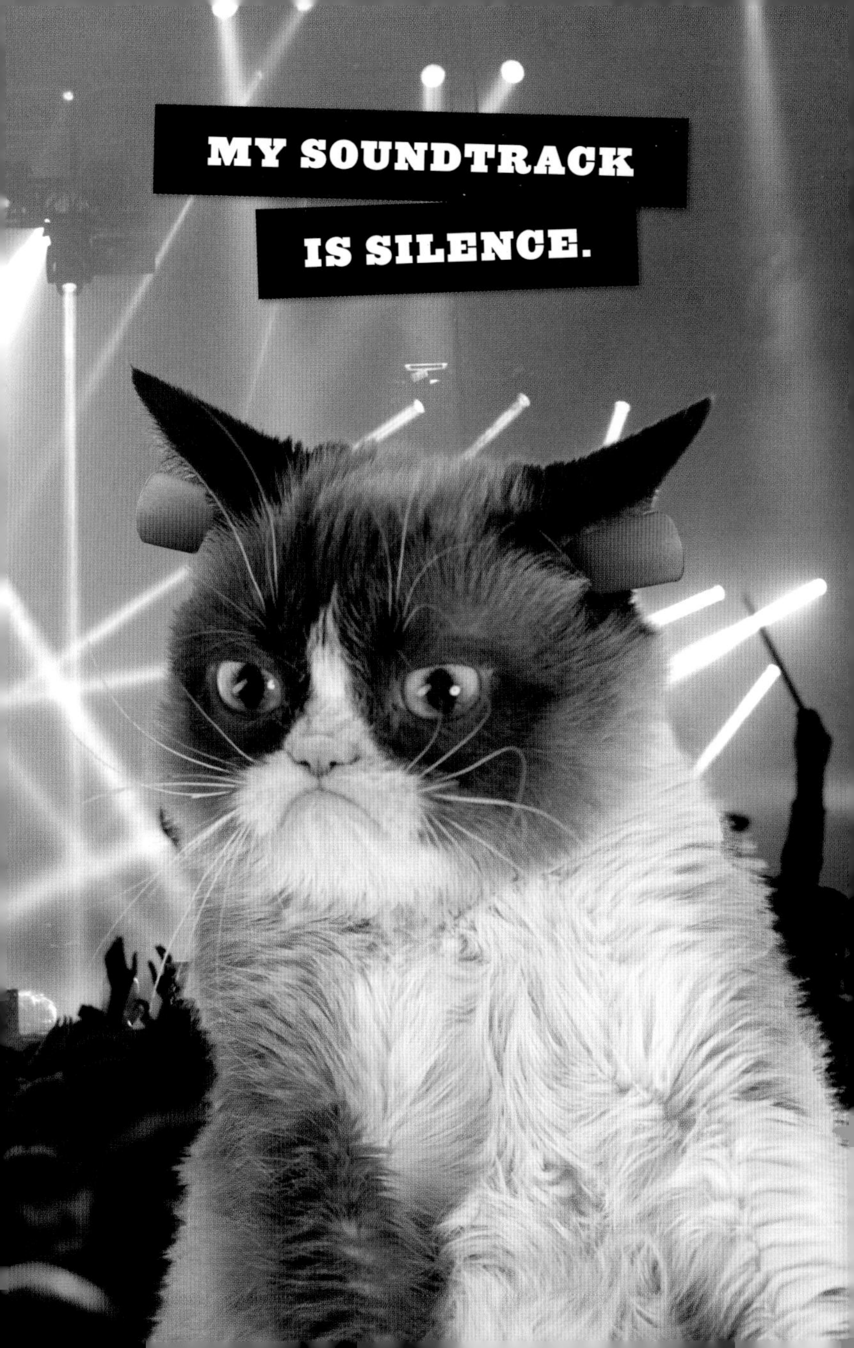
MY SOUNDTRACK
IS SILENCE.

Television

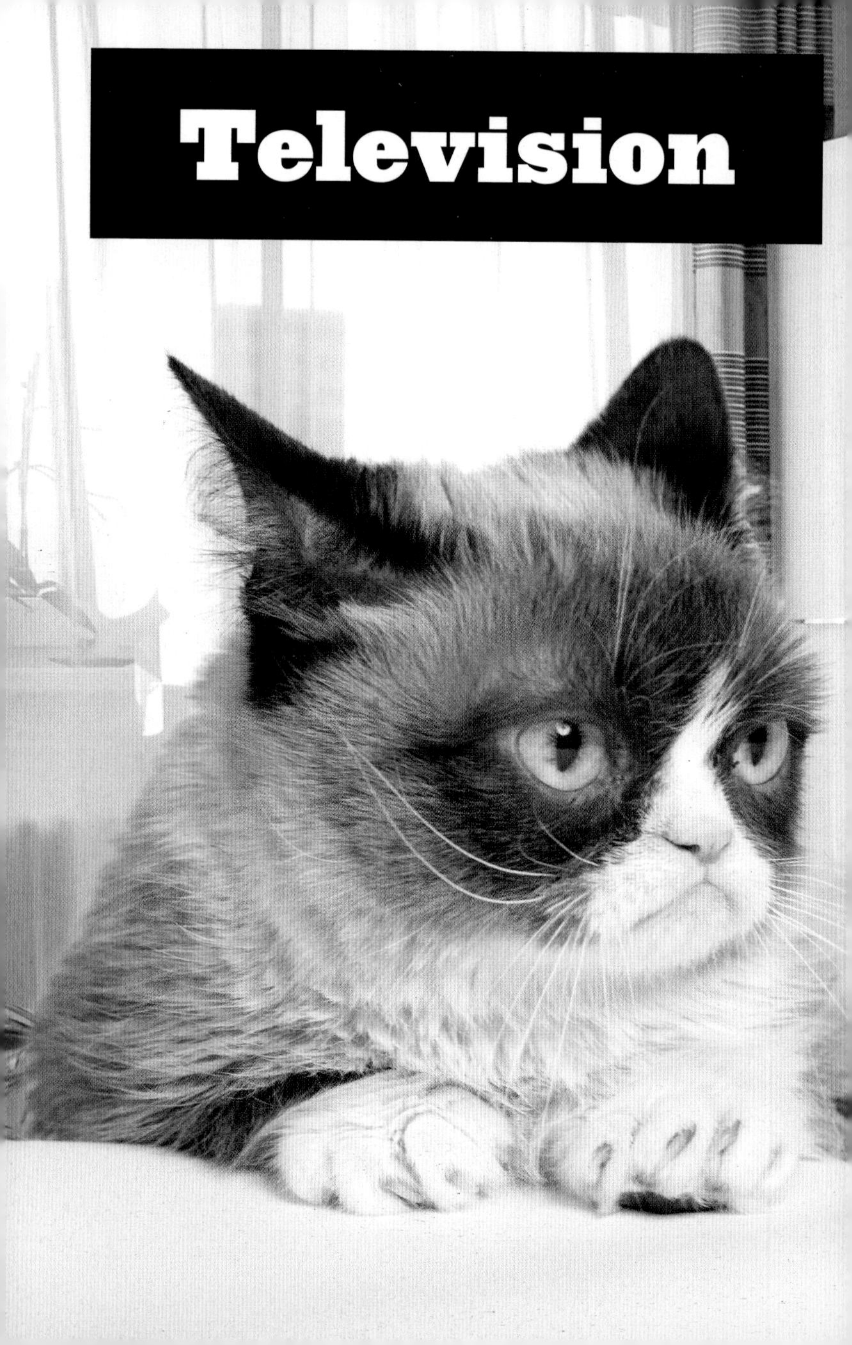

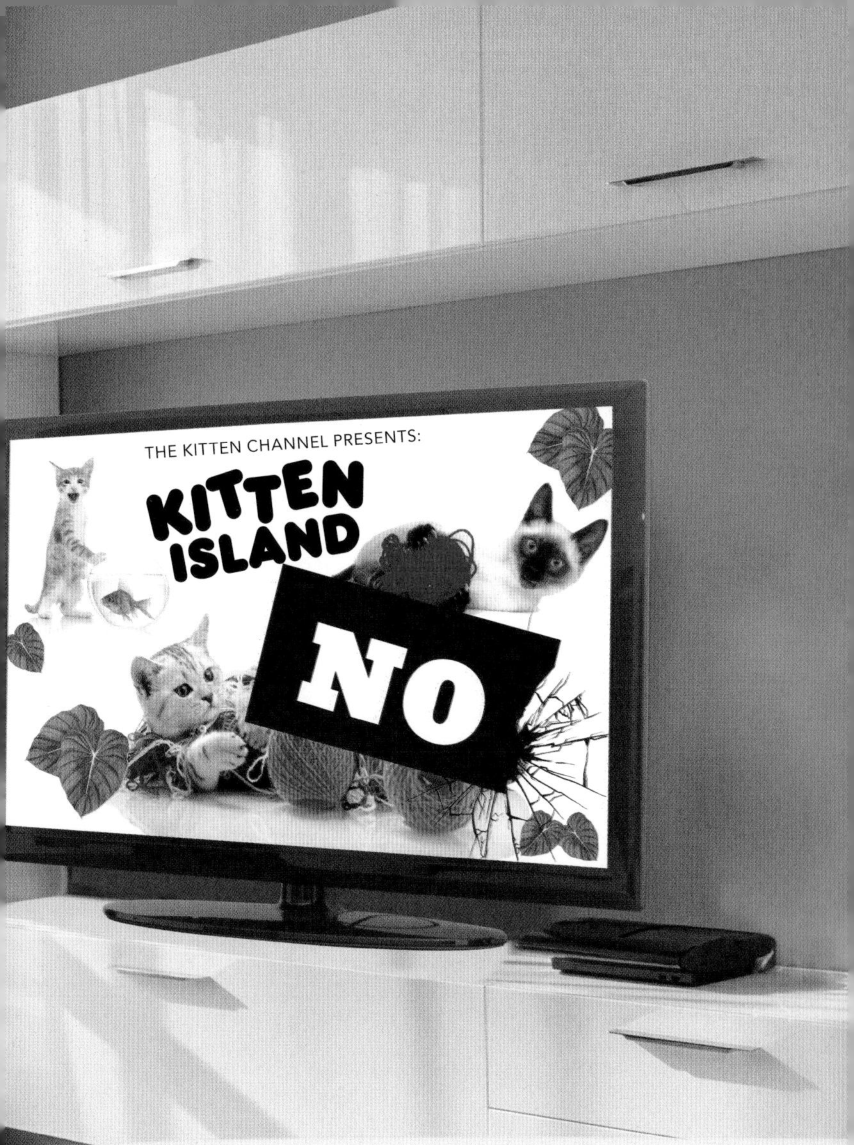
THE KITTEN CHANNEL PRESENTS:
KITTEN ISLAND
NO

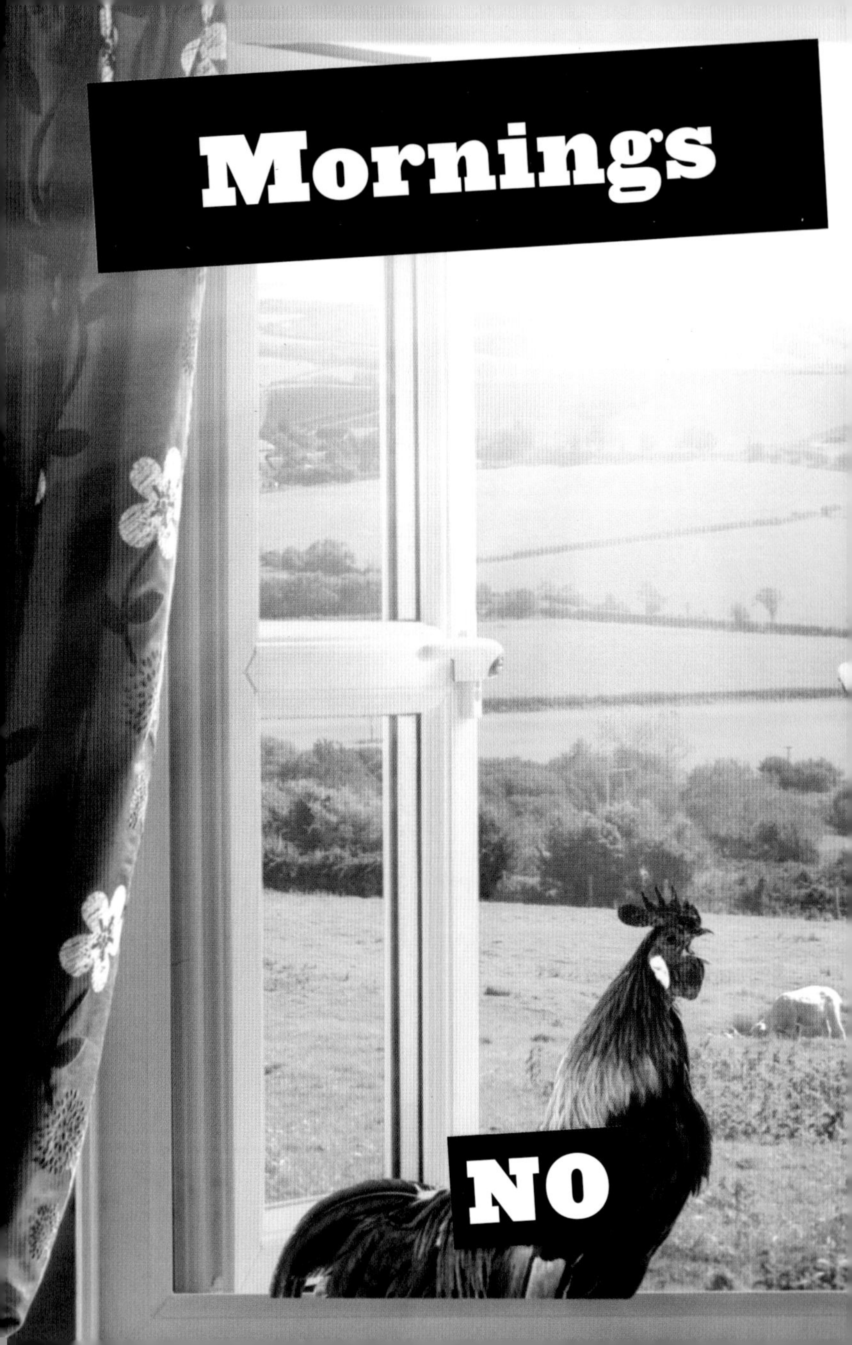
Mornings
NO

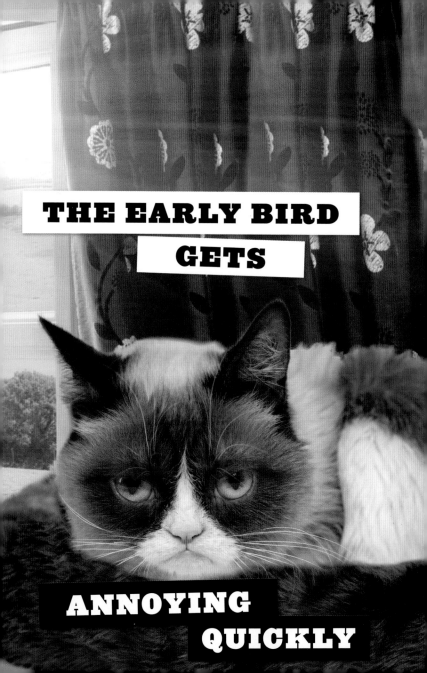

THE EARLY BIRD
GETS

ANNOYING
QUICKLY

Sequels

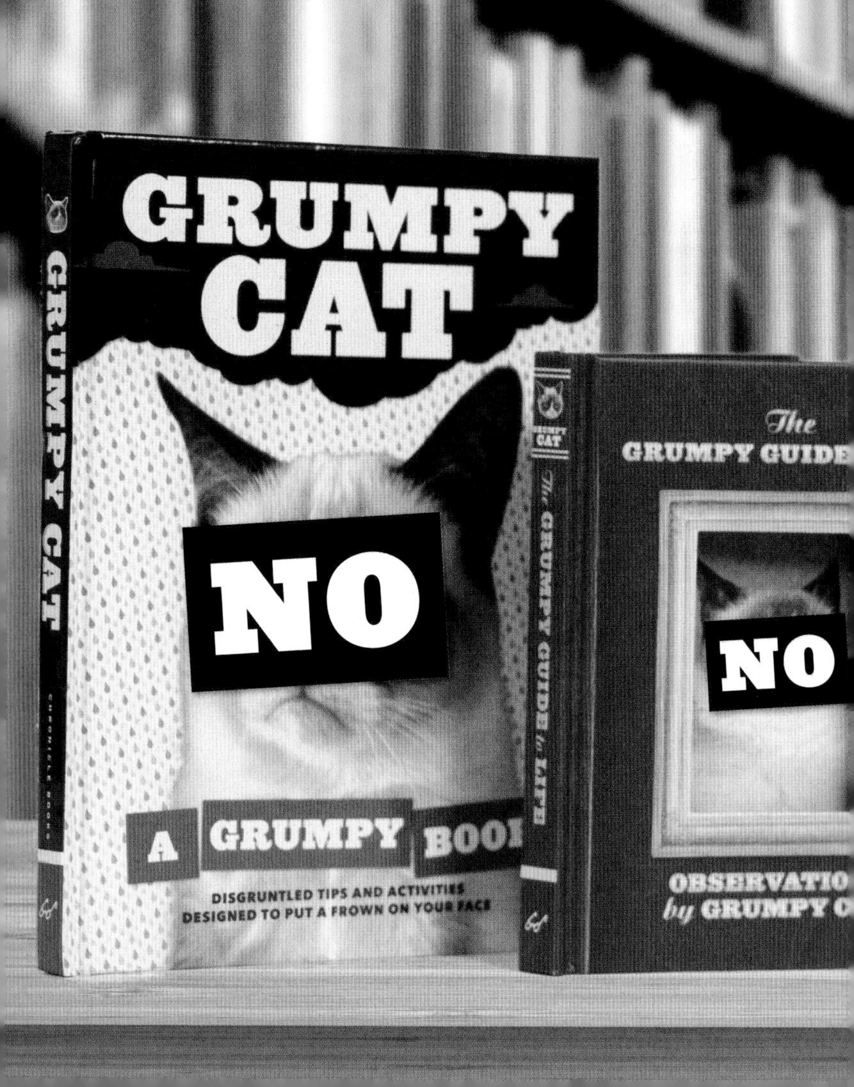
GRUMPY CAT
NO
A GRUMPY BOOK
DISGRUNTLED TIPS AND ACTIVITIES DESIGNED TO PUT A FROWN ON YOUR FACE
GRUMPY CAT
The GRUMPY GUIDE to LIFE
The GRUMPY GUIDE
NO

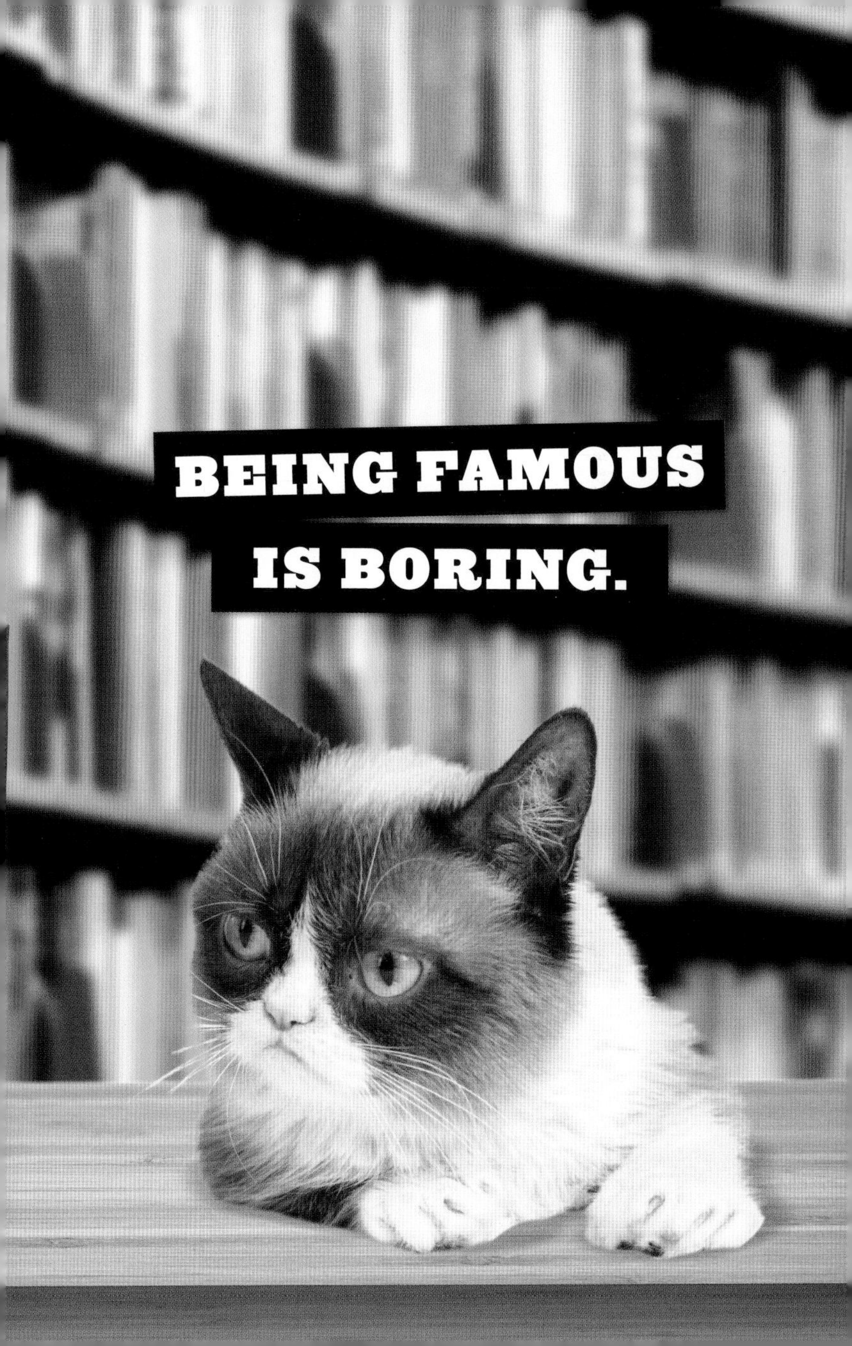
BEING FAMOUS
IS BORING.

Kittens

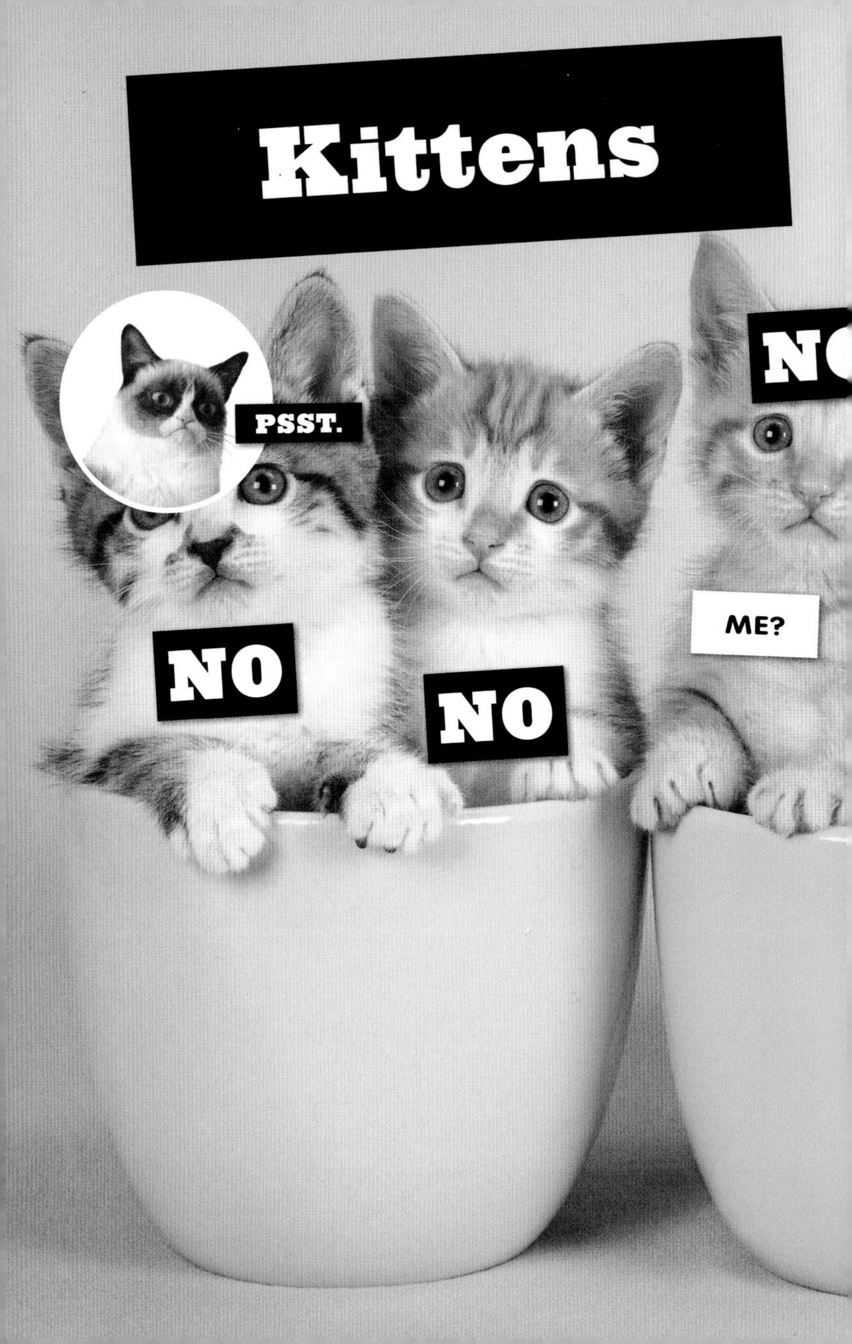

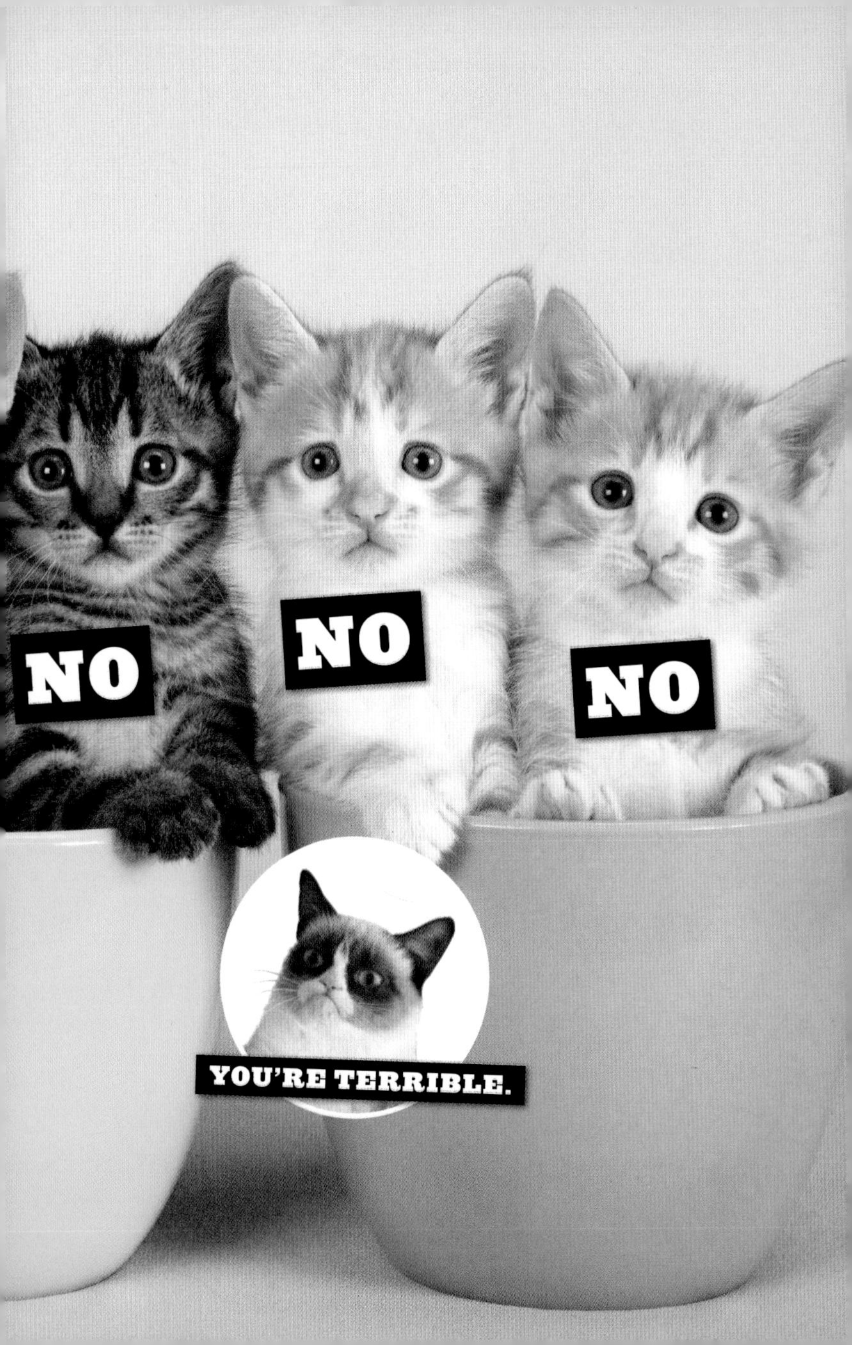
NO
NO
NO
YOU'RE TERRIBLE.

Dogs

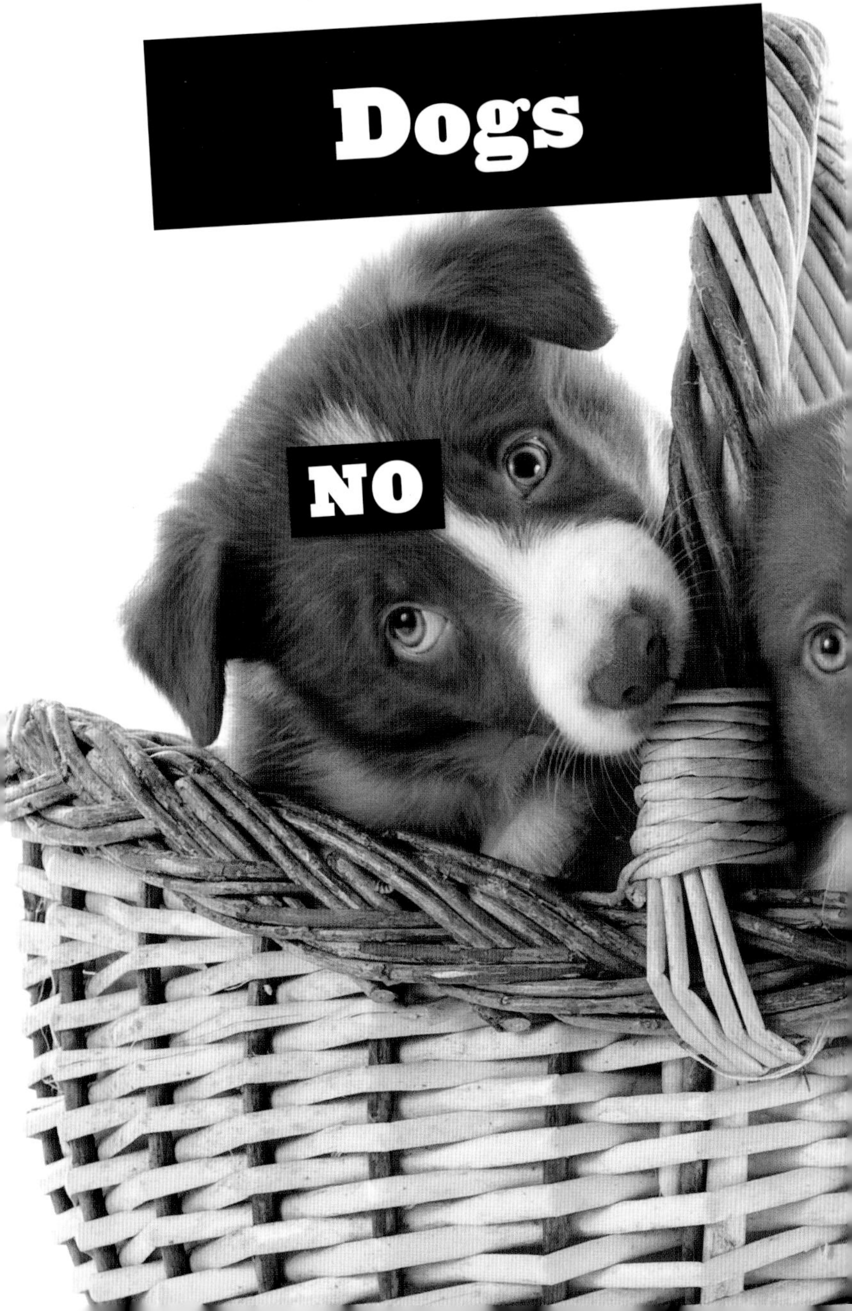

NO

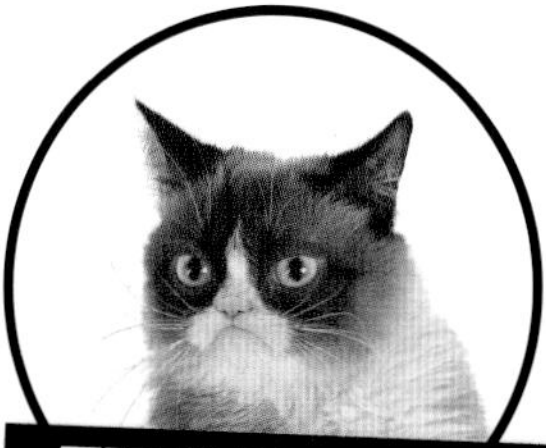

THIS IS WHAT
A BASKET OF
BAD BREATH
LOOKS LIKE.

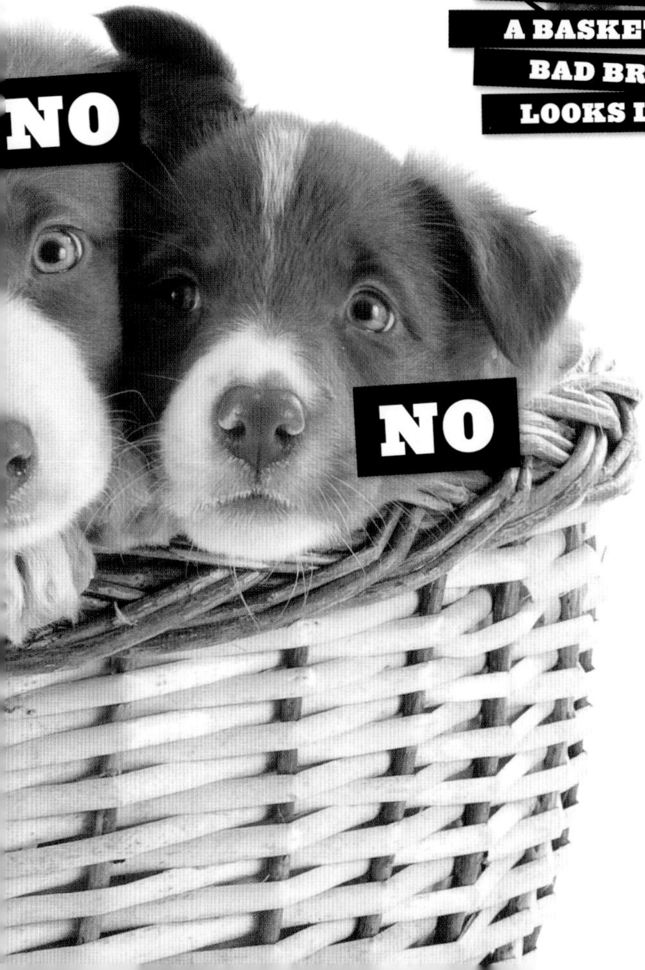
NO
NO

Any Cute Animals, Really

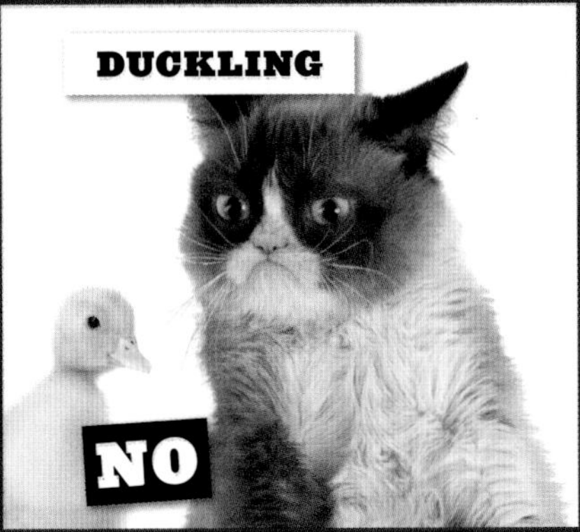
DUCKLING
NO

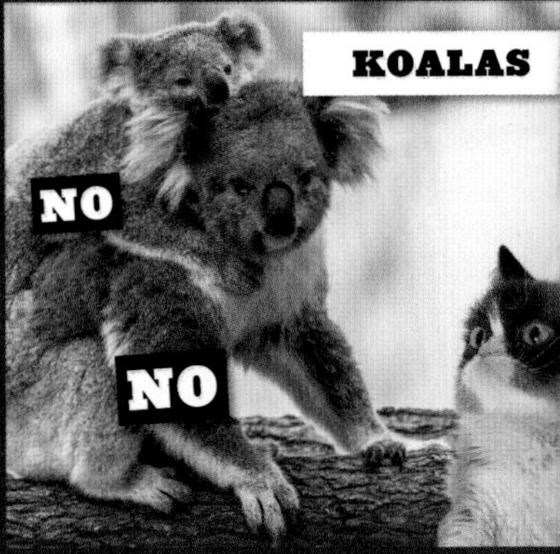
KOALAS
NO
NO

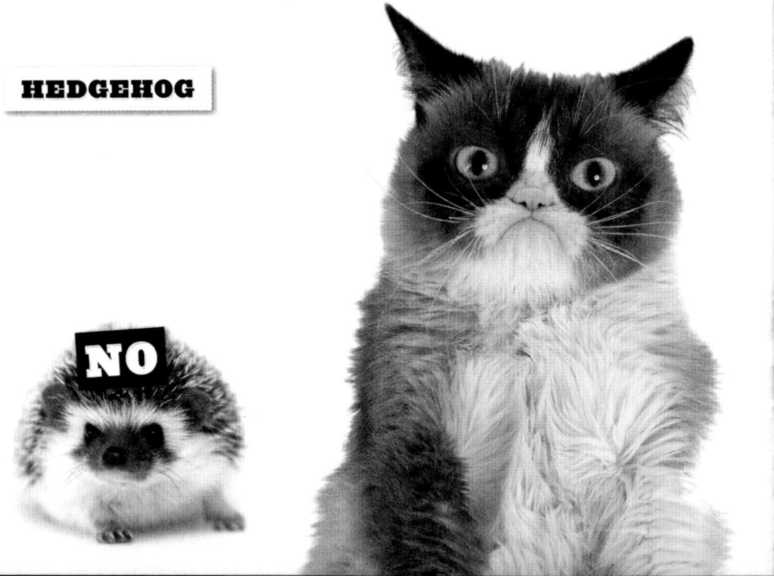
HEDGEHOG
NO

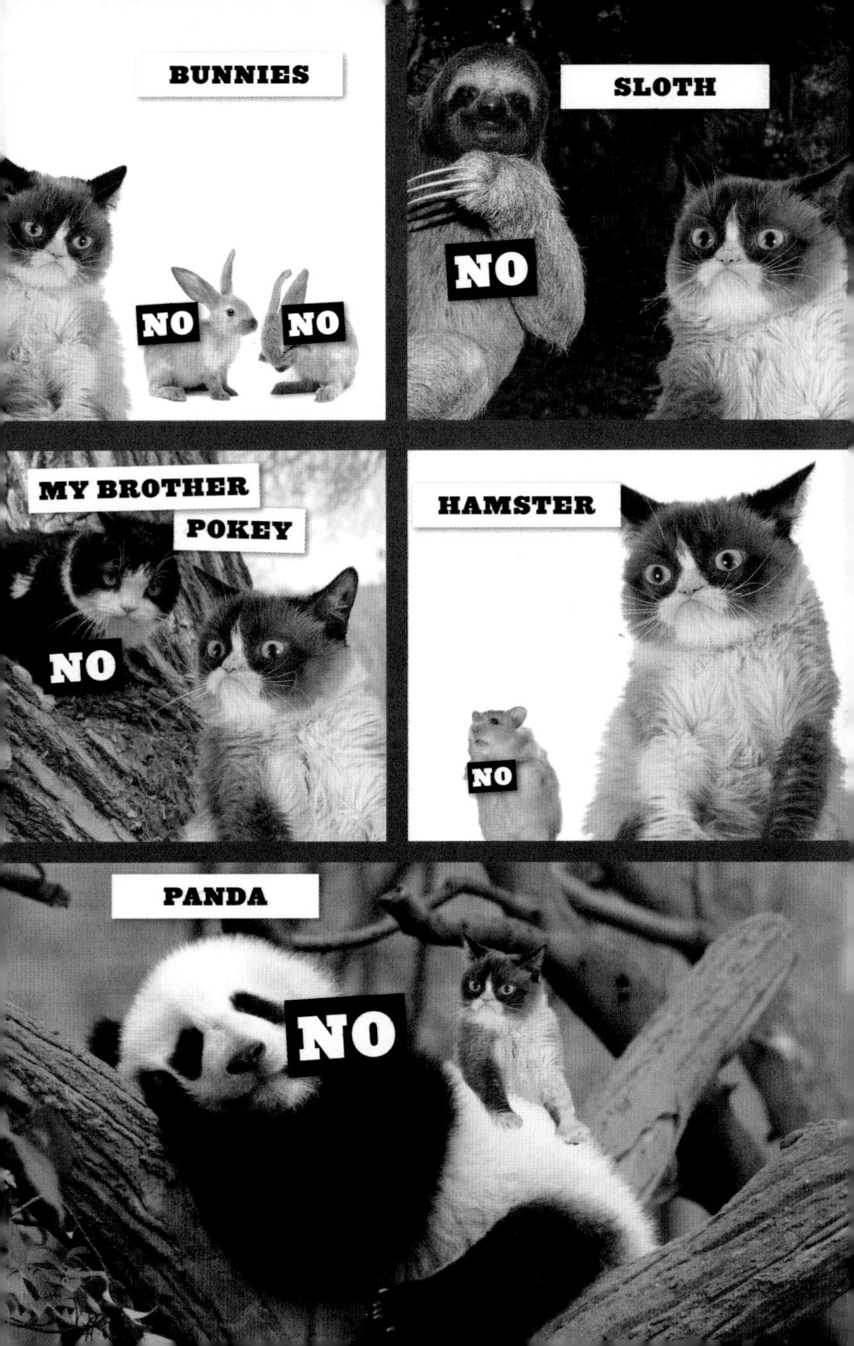
BUNNIES
NO
NO
SLOTH
NO
MY BROTHER
POKEY
NO
HAMSTER
NO
PANDA
NO

The Internet

NO 🔍

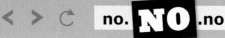

THINKING OF YOU

IT'S TERRIBLE

IF YOU'RE HAPPY AND YOU KNOW IT

GET AWAY FROM ME

I HAD FUN

IT WAS AW

FROWN AND THE WHOLE WORLD FROWNS WITH YOU.

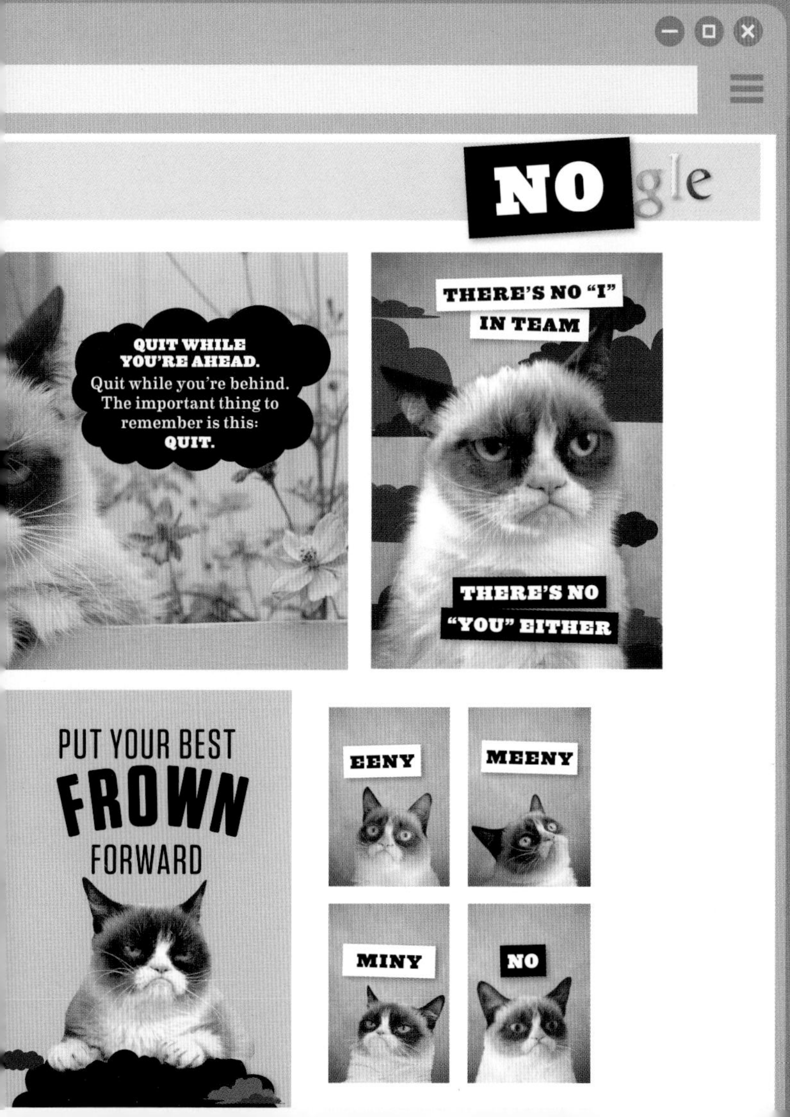
NO gle
QUIT WHILE YOU'RE AHEAD.
Quit while you're behind.
The important thing to remember is this:
QUIT.
THERE'S NO "I" IN TEAM
THERE'S NO "YOU" EITHER
PUT YOUR BEST FROWN FORWARD
EENY
MEENY
MINY
NO

Magic

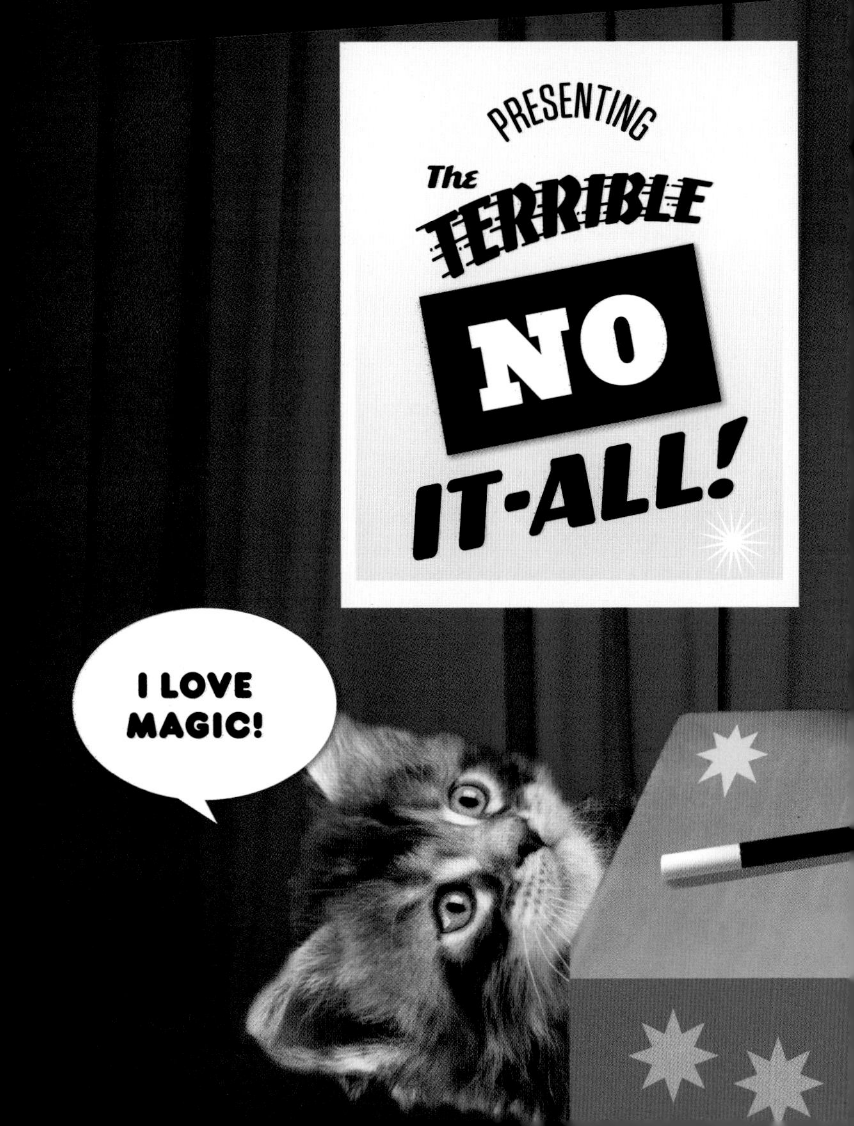
PRESENTING
The TERRIBLE
NO
IT-ALL!
I LOVE MAGIC!

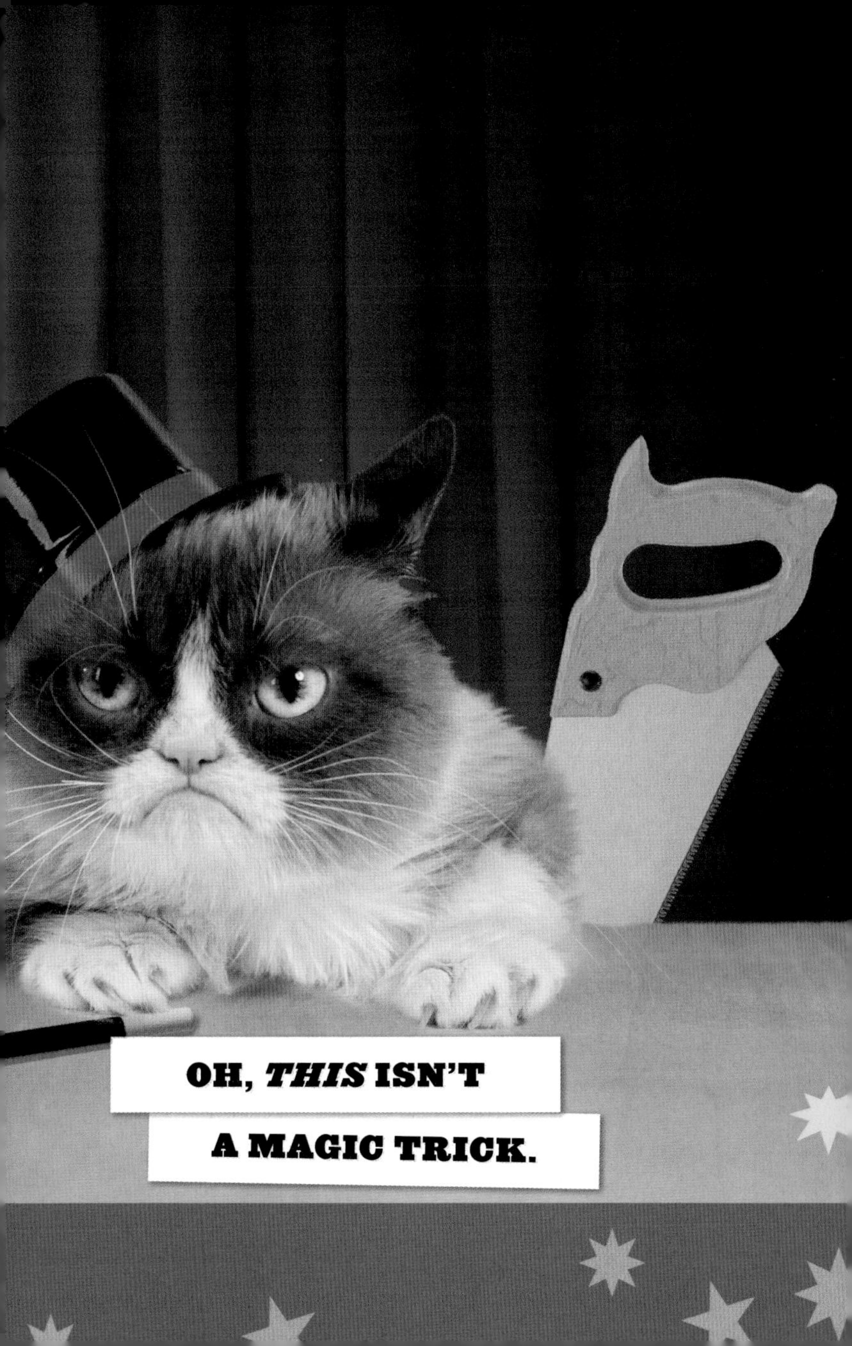
OH, *THIS* ISN'T
A MAGIC TRICK.

Balloons

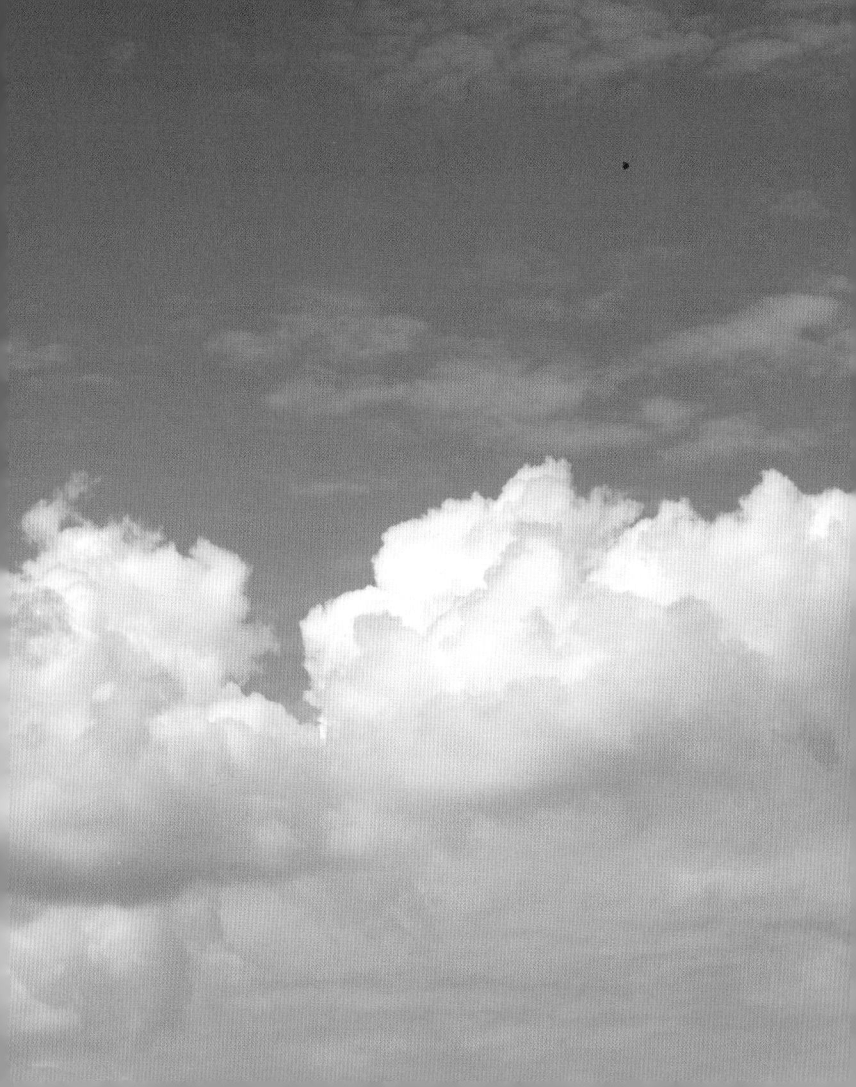

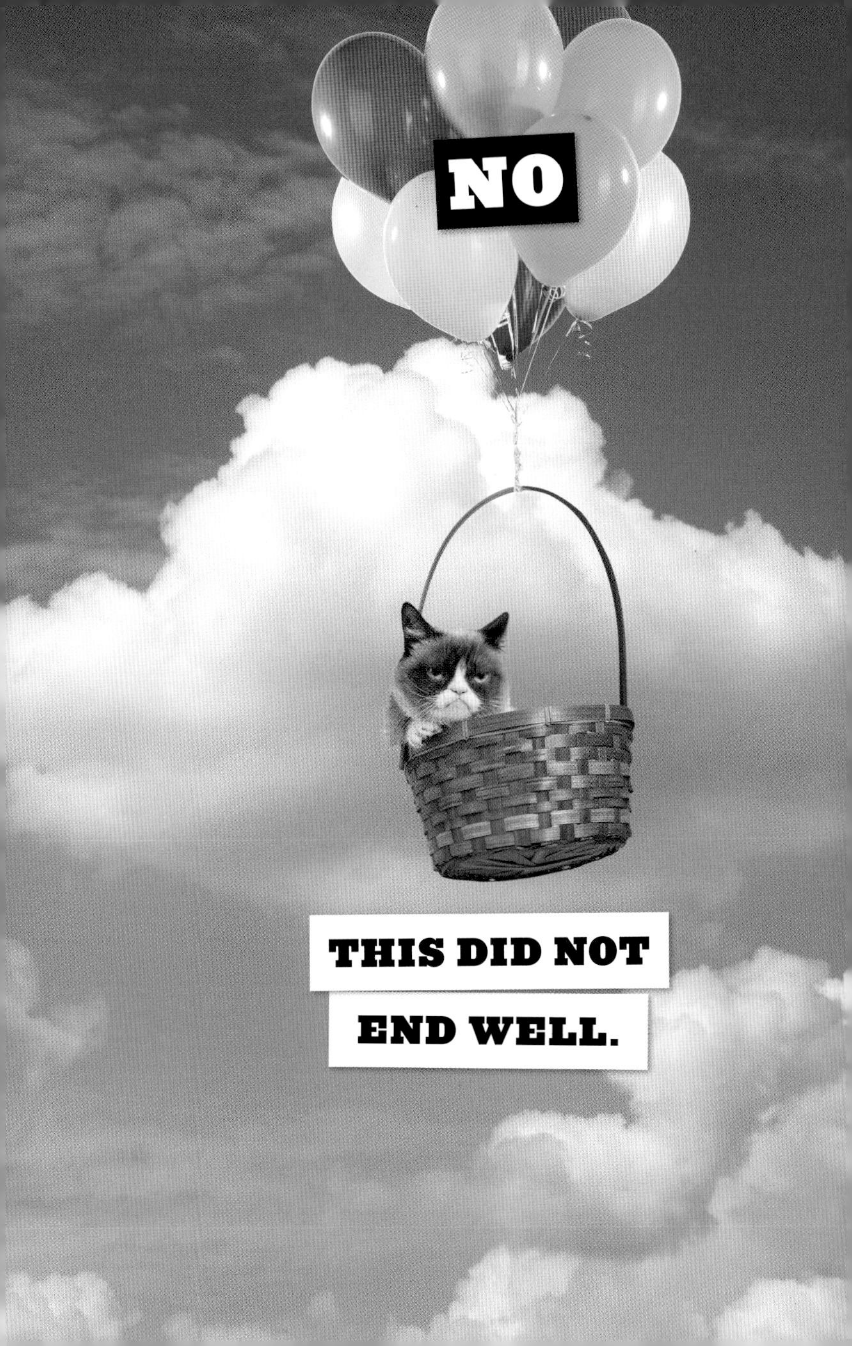
NO
THIS DID NOT
END WELL.

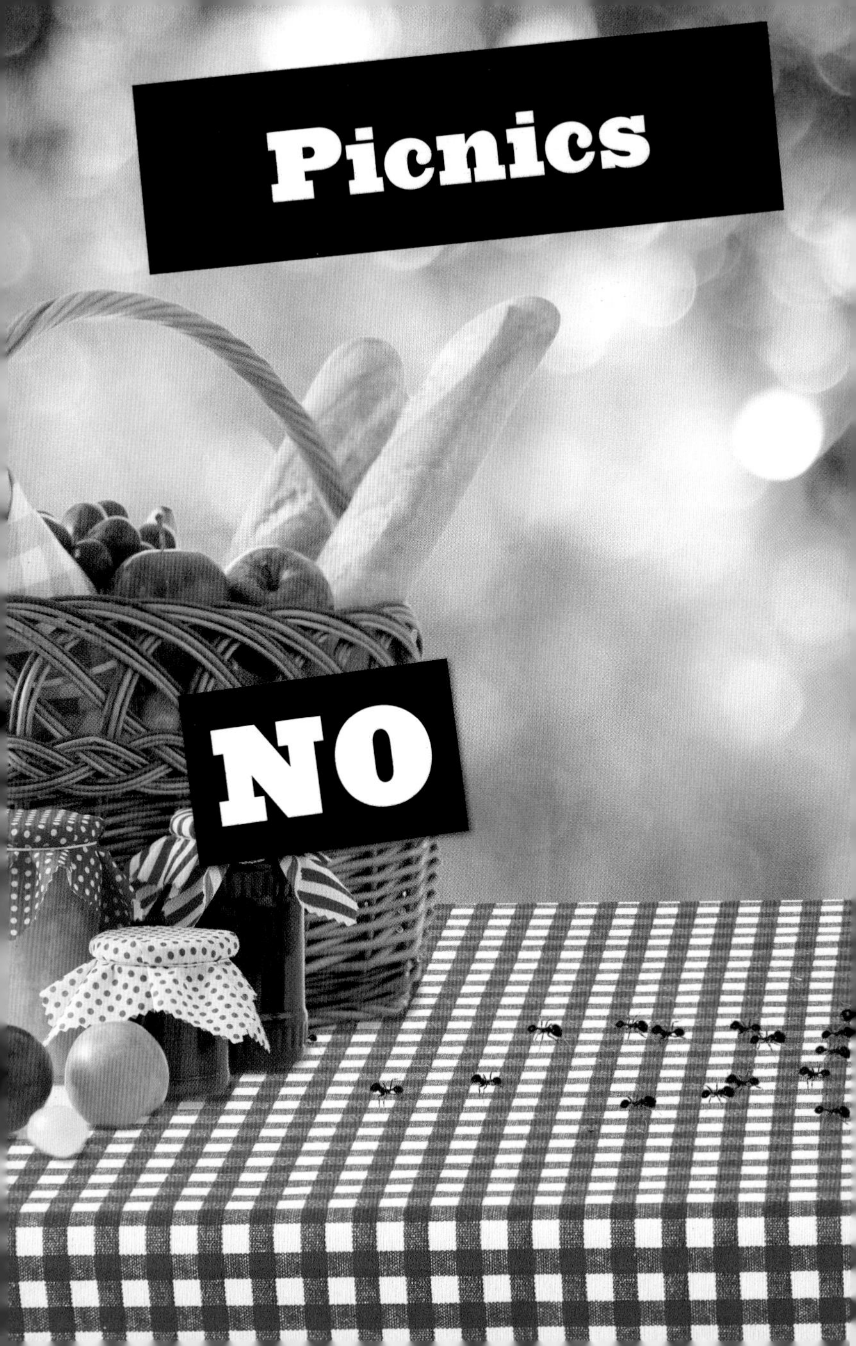
Picnics
NO

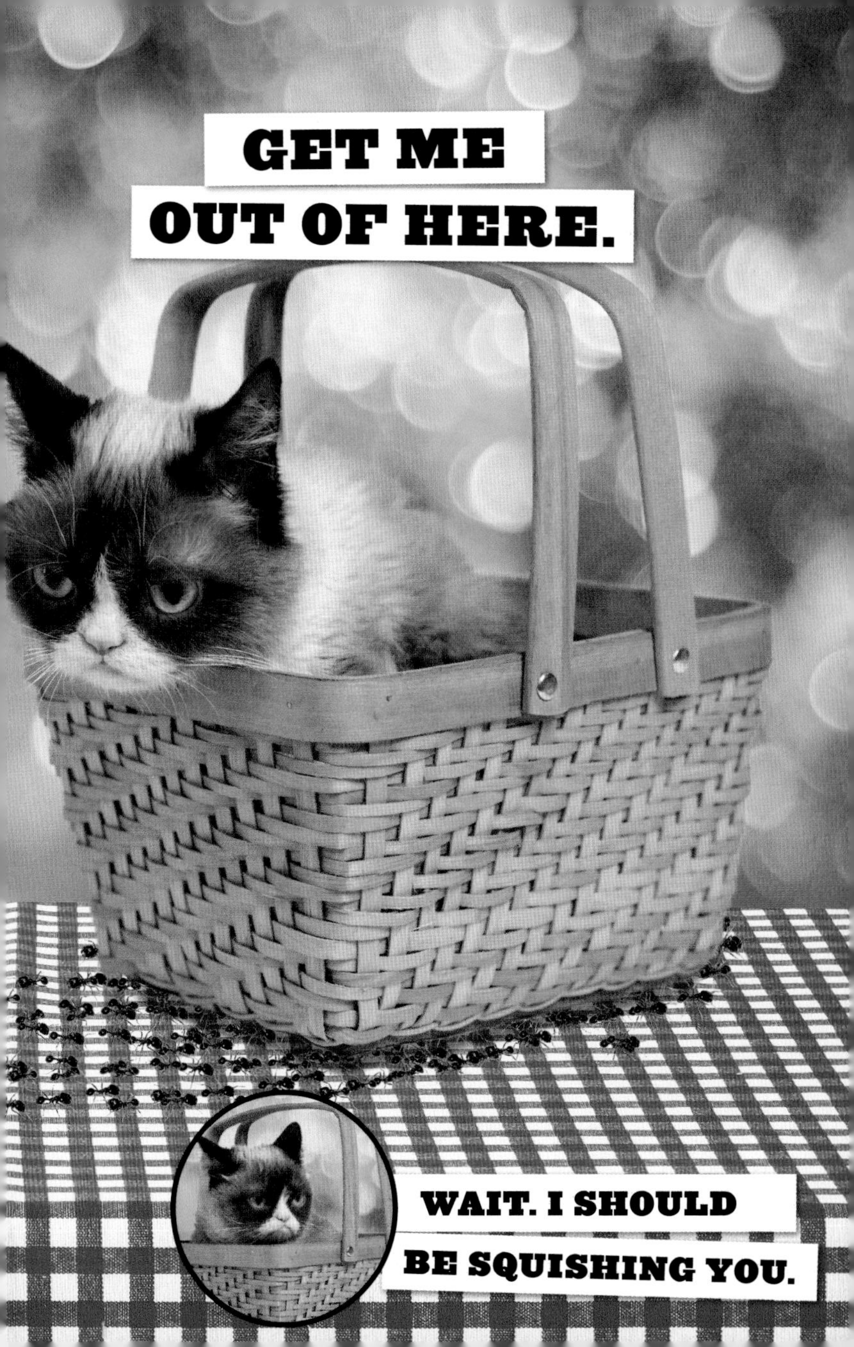
GET ME
OUT OF HERE.
WAIT. I SHOULD
BE SQUISHING YOU.

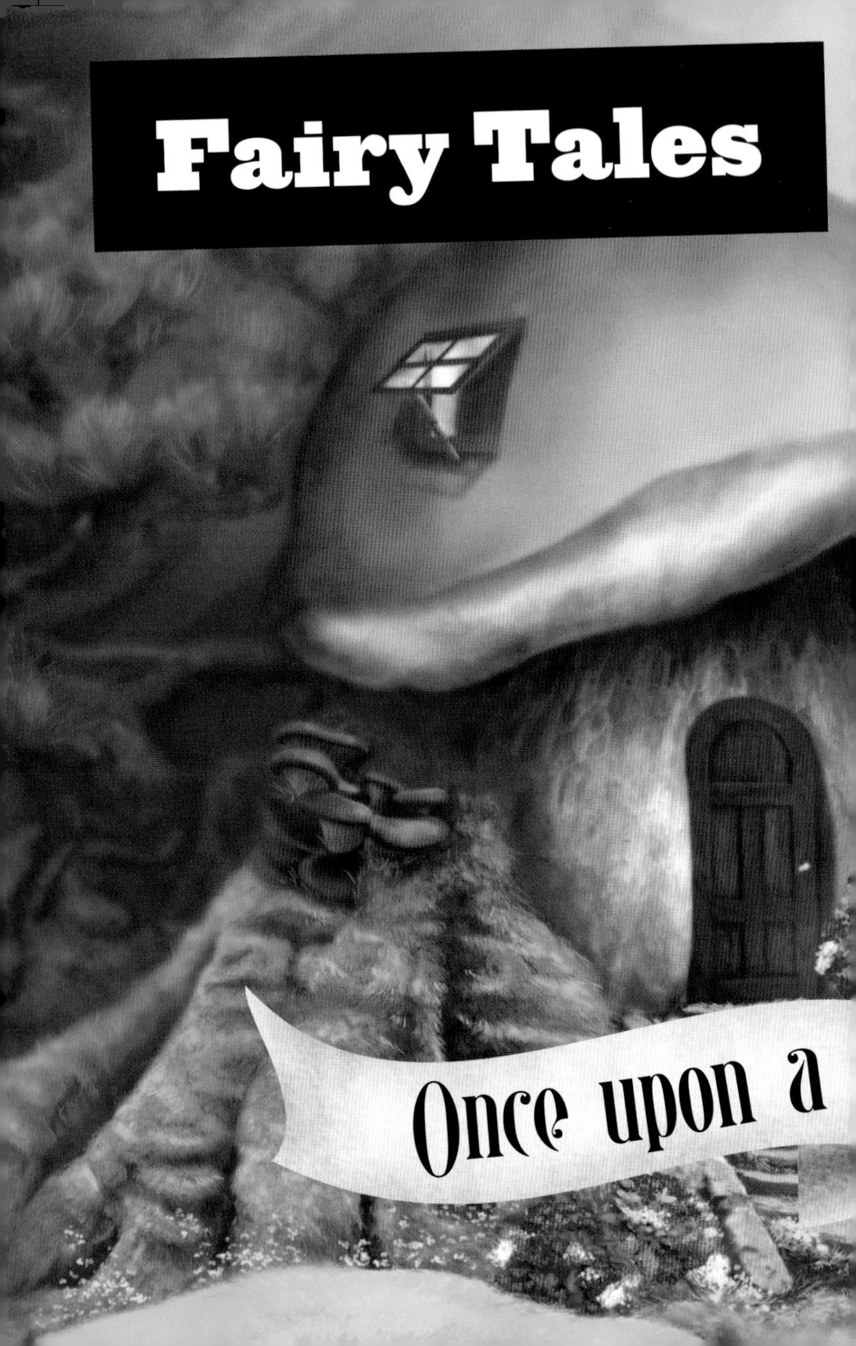
Fairy Tales
Once upon a

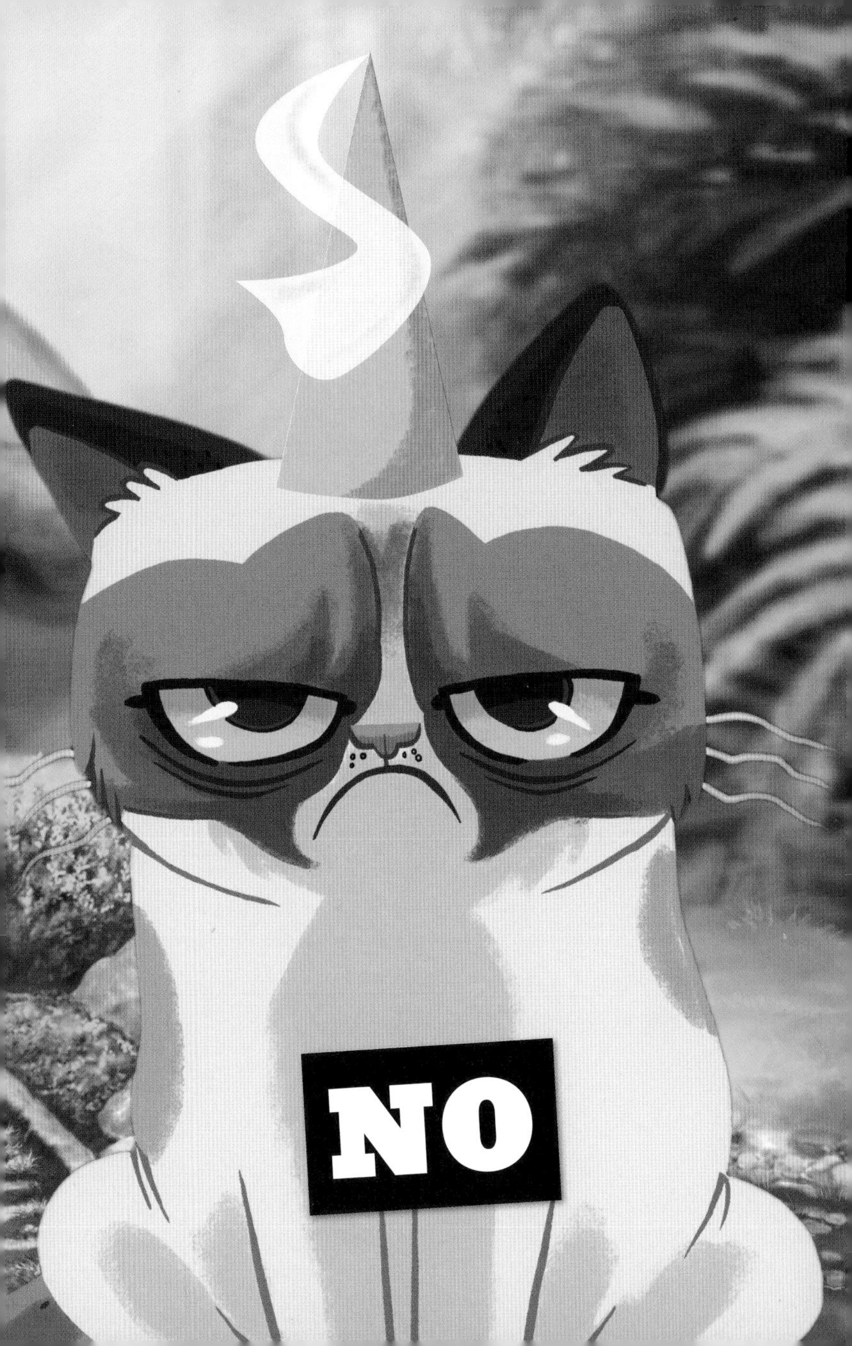
NO

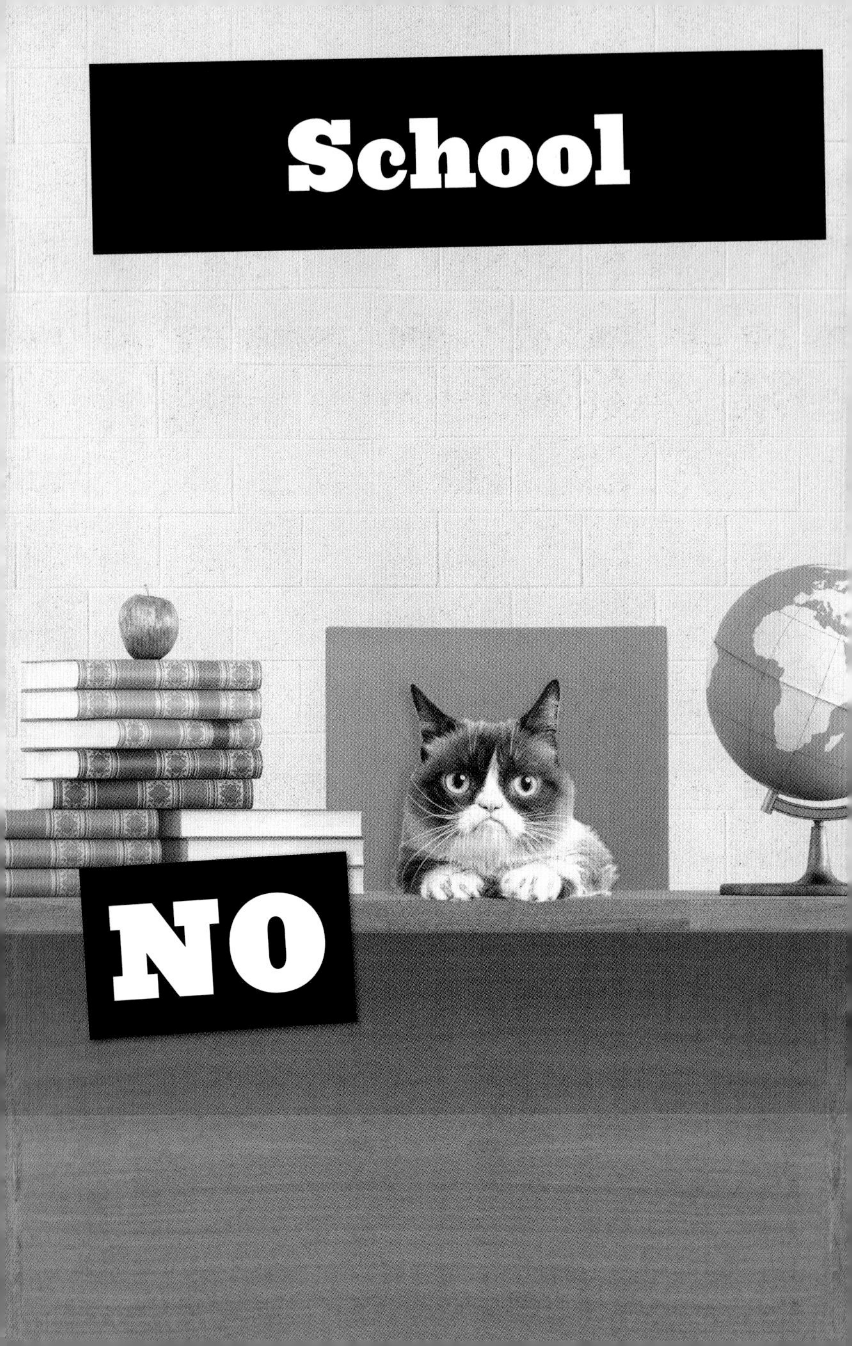
School
NO

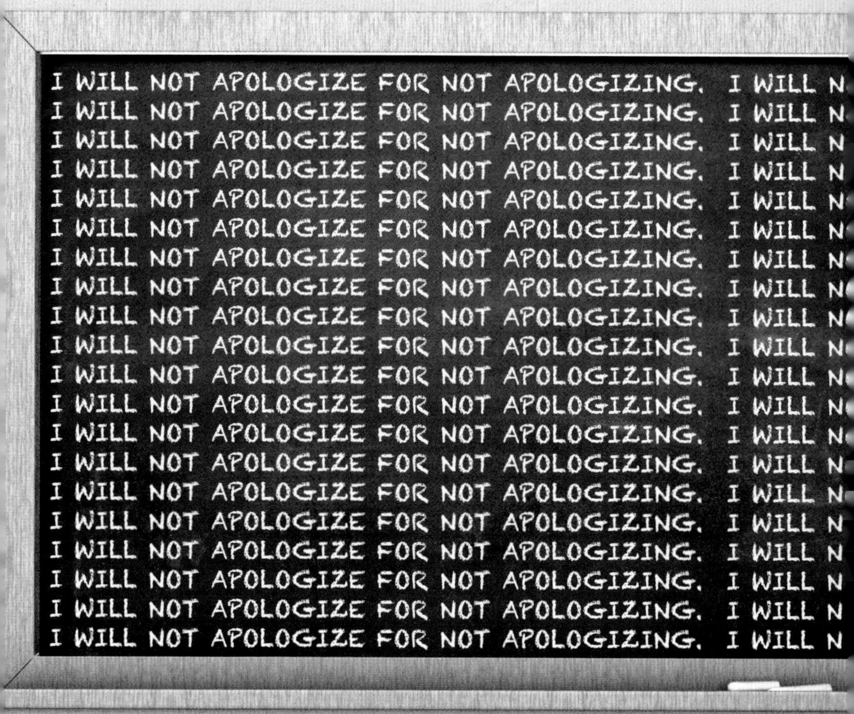

I WILL NOT APOLOGIZE FOR NOT APOLOGIZING. I WILL N
I WILL NOT APOLOGIZE FOR NOT APOLOGIZING. I WILL N
I WILL NOT APOLOGIZE FOR NOT APOLOGIZING. I WILL N
I WILL NOT APOLOGIZE FOR NOT APOLOGIZING. I WILL N
I WILL NOT APOLOGIZE FOR NOT APOLOGIZING. I WILL N
I WILL NOT APOLOGIZE FOR NOT APOLOGIZING. I WILL N
I WILL NOT APOLOGIZE FOR NOT APOLOGIZING. I WILL N
I WILL NOT APOLOGIZE FOR NOT APOLOGIZING. I WILL N
I WILL NOT APOLOGIZE FOR NOT APOLOGIZING. I WILL N
I WILL NOT APOLOGIZE FOR NOT APOLOGIZING. I WILL N
I WILL NOT APOLOGIZE FOR NOT APOLOGIZING. I WILL N
I WILL NOT APOLOGIZE FOR NOT APOLOGIZING. I WILL N
I WILL NOT APOLOGIZE FOR NOT APOLOGIZING. I WILL N
I WILL NOT APOLOGIZE FOR NOT APOLOGIZING. I WILL N
I WILL NOT APOLOGIZE FOR NOT APOLOGIZING. I WILL N
I WILL NOT APOLOGIZE FOR NOT APOLOGIZING. I WILL N
I WILL NOT APOLOGIZE FOR NOT APOLOGIZING. I WILL N
I WILL NOT APOLOGIZE FOR NOT APOLOGIZING. I WILL N
I WILL NOT APOLOGIZE FOR NOT APOLOGIZING. I WILL N
I WILL NOT APOLOGIZE FOR NOT APOLOGIZING. I WILL N

MY HOMEWORK

ATE THE DOG.

Dreams

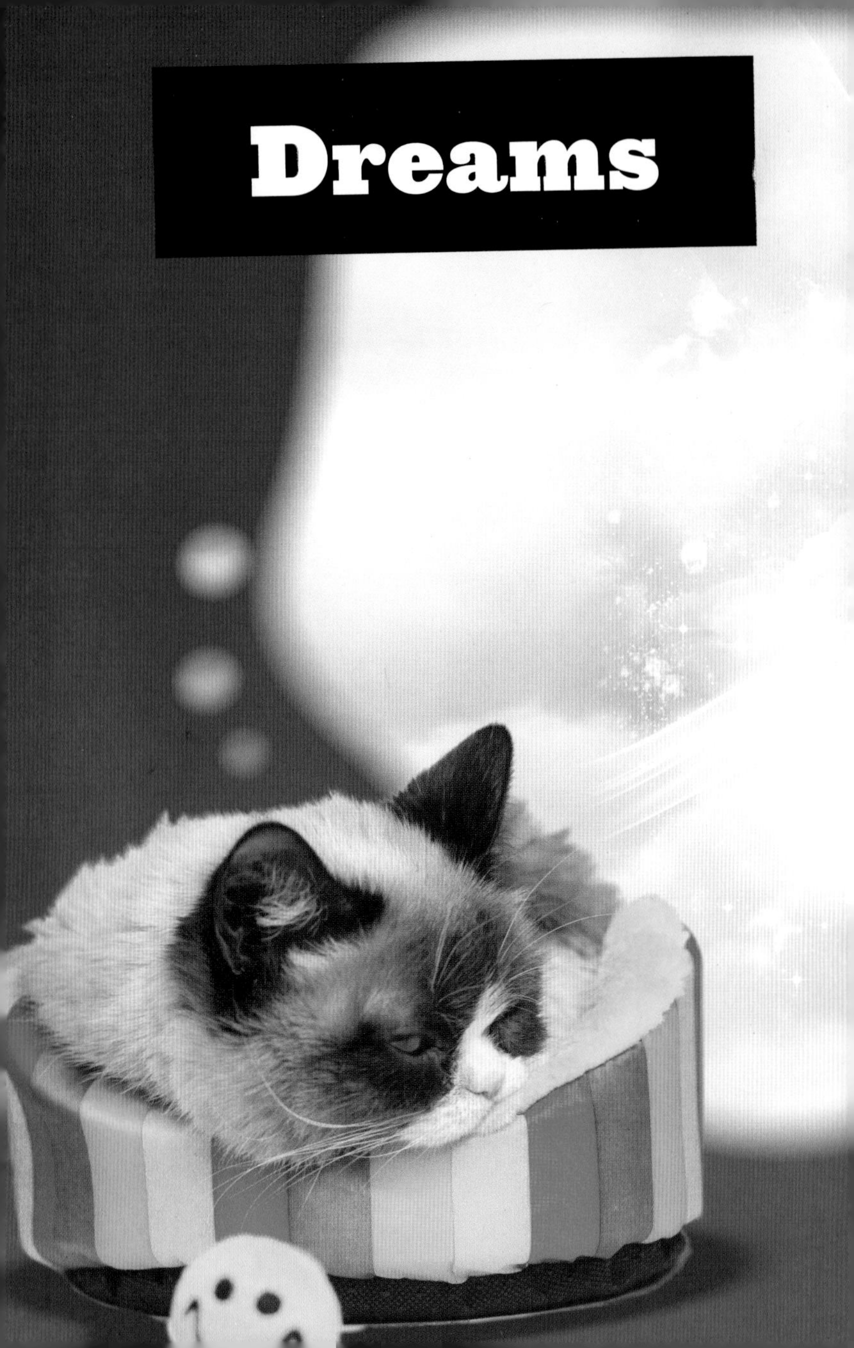

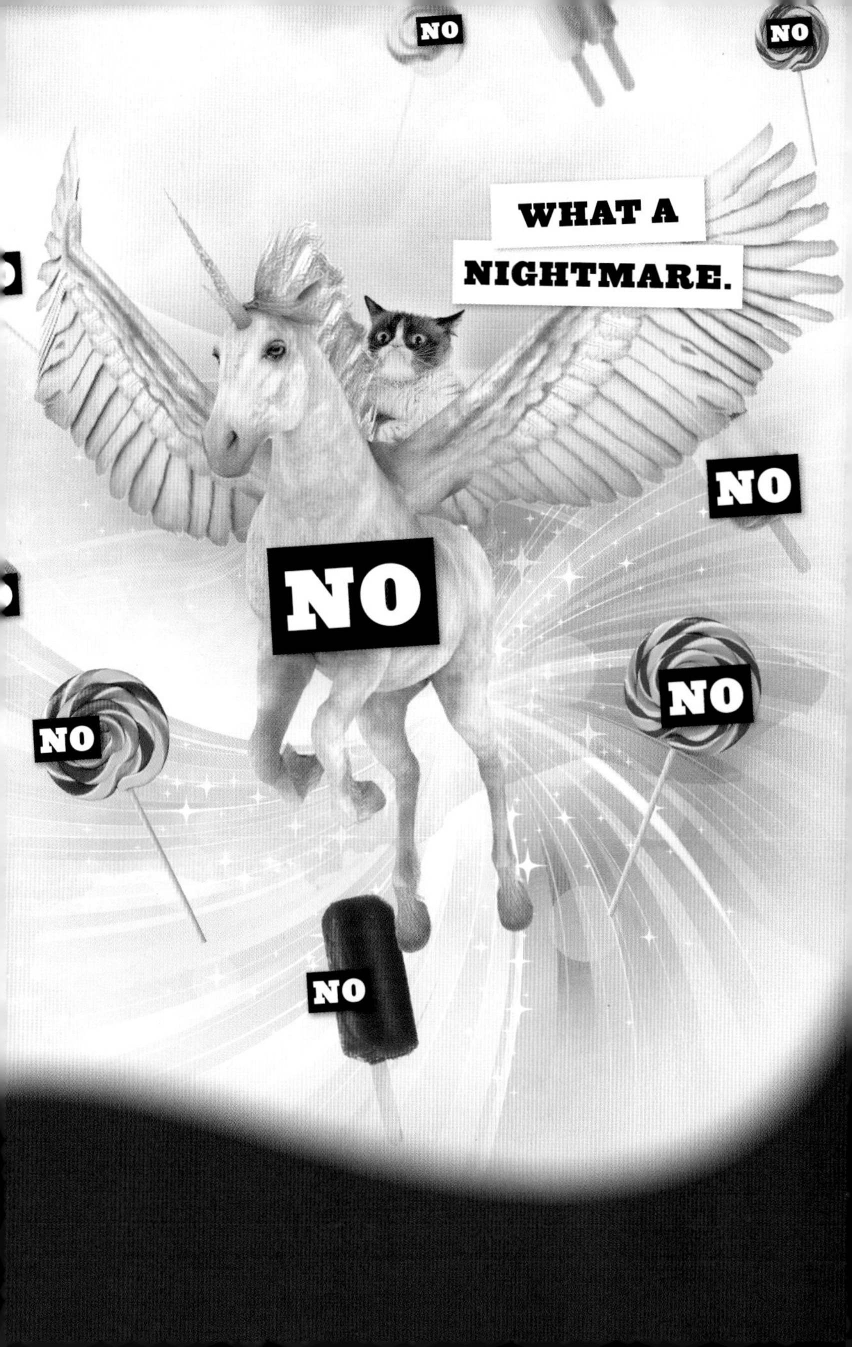
NO
NO
WHAT A
NIGHTMARE.
NO
NO
NO
NO
NO

Crowds

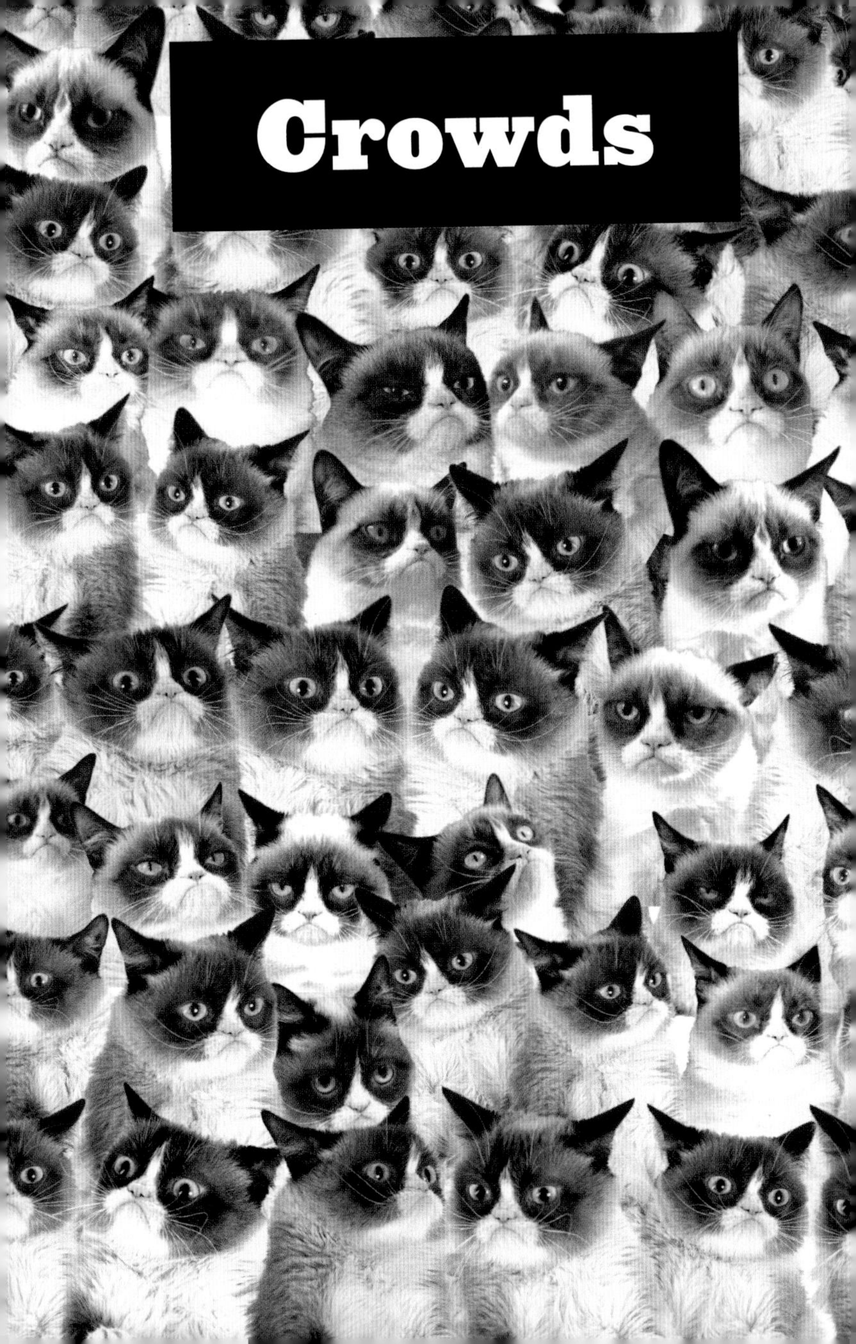

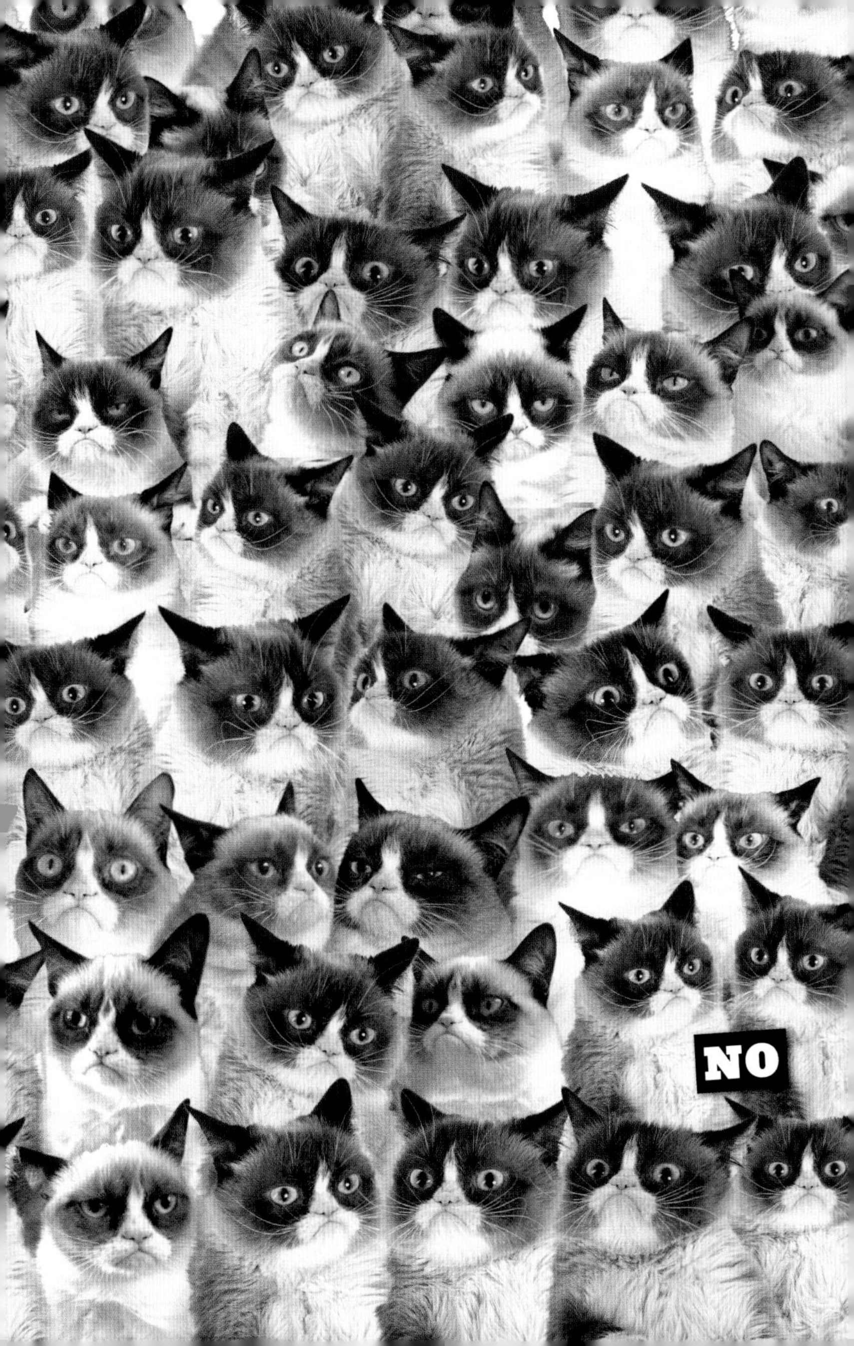
NO

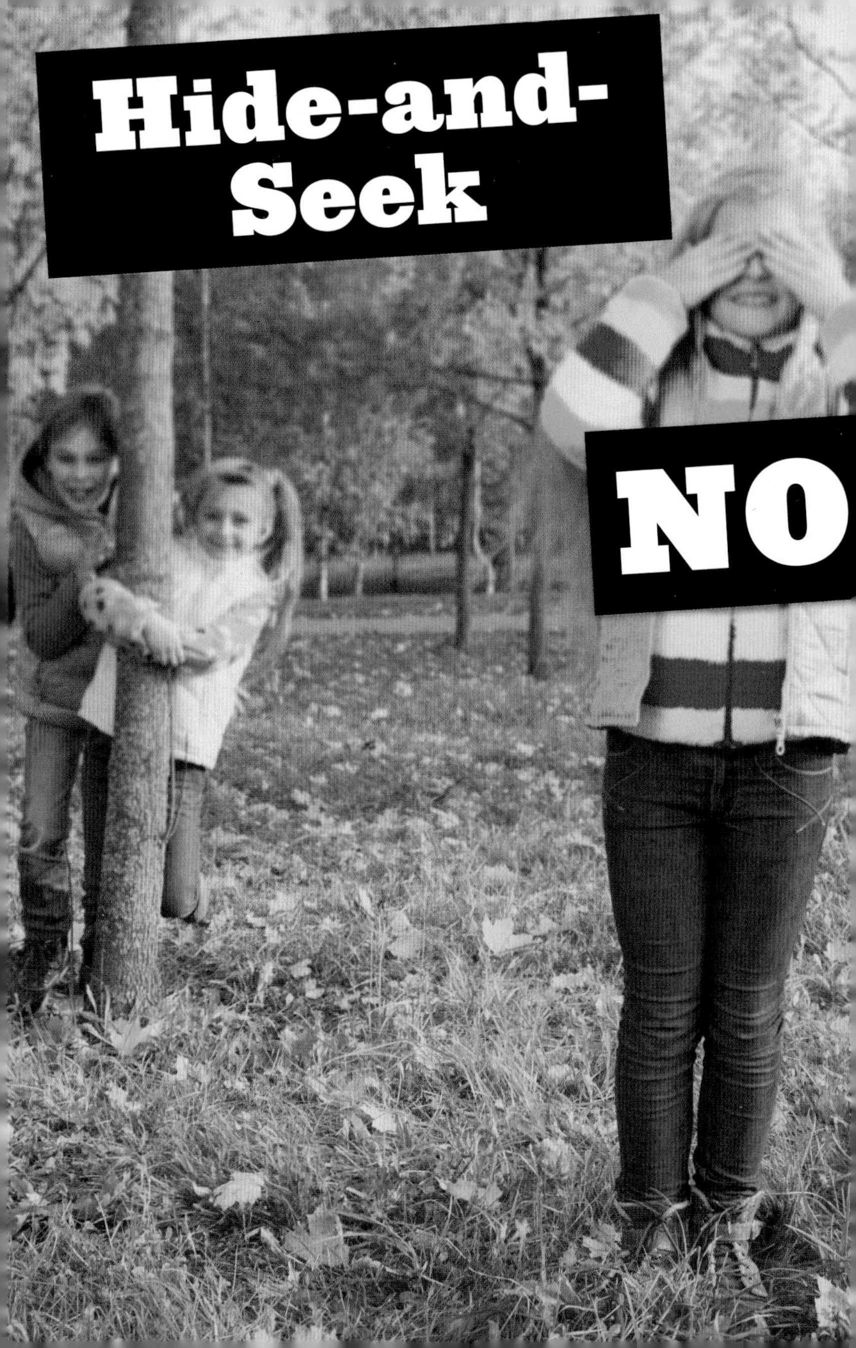
Hide-and-Seek
NO

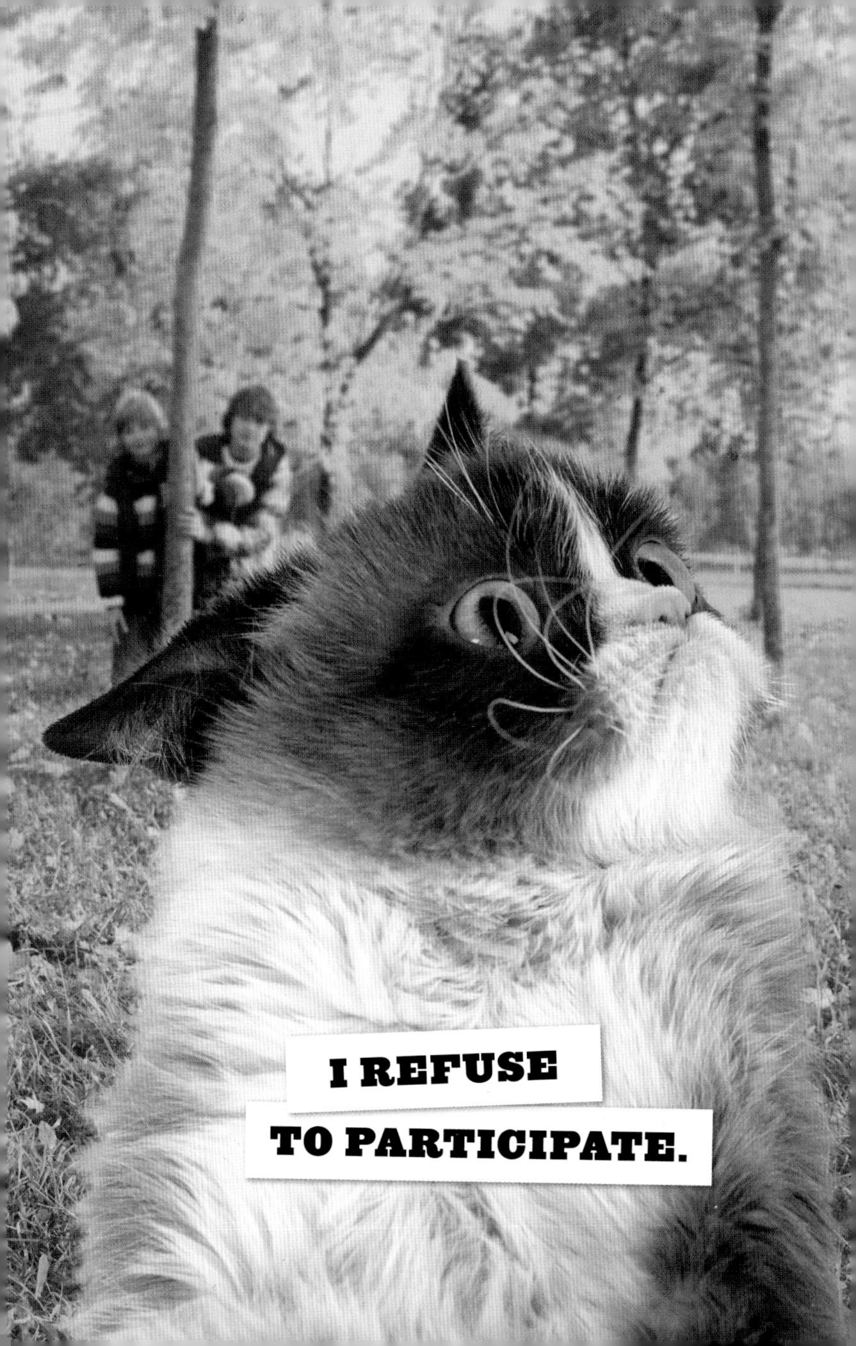
I REFUSE
TO PARTICIPATE.

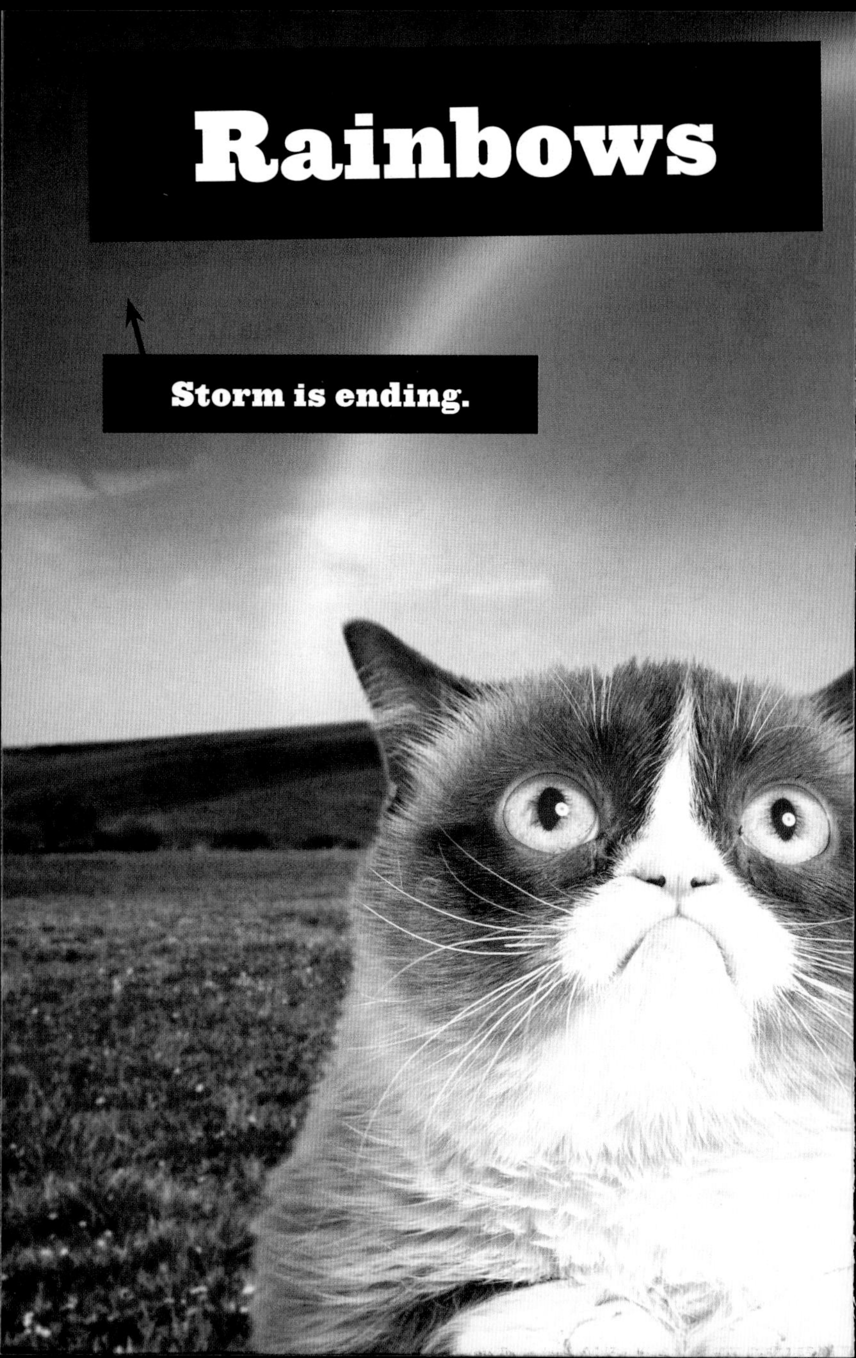
Rainbows
Storm is ending.

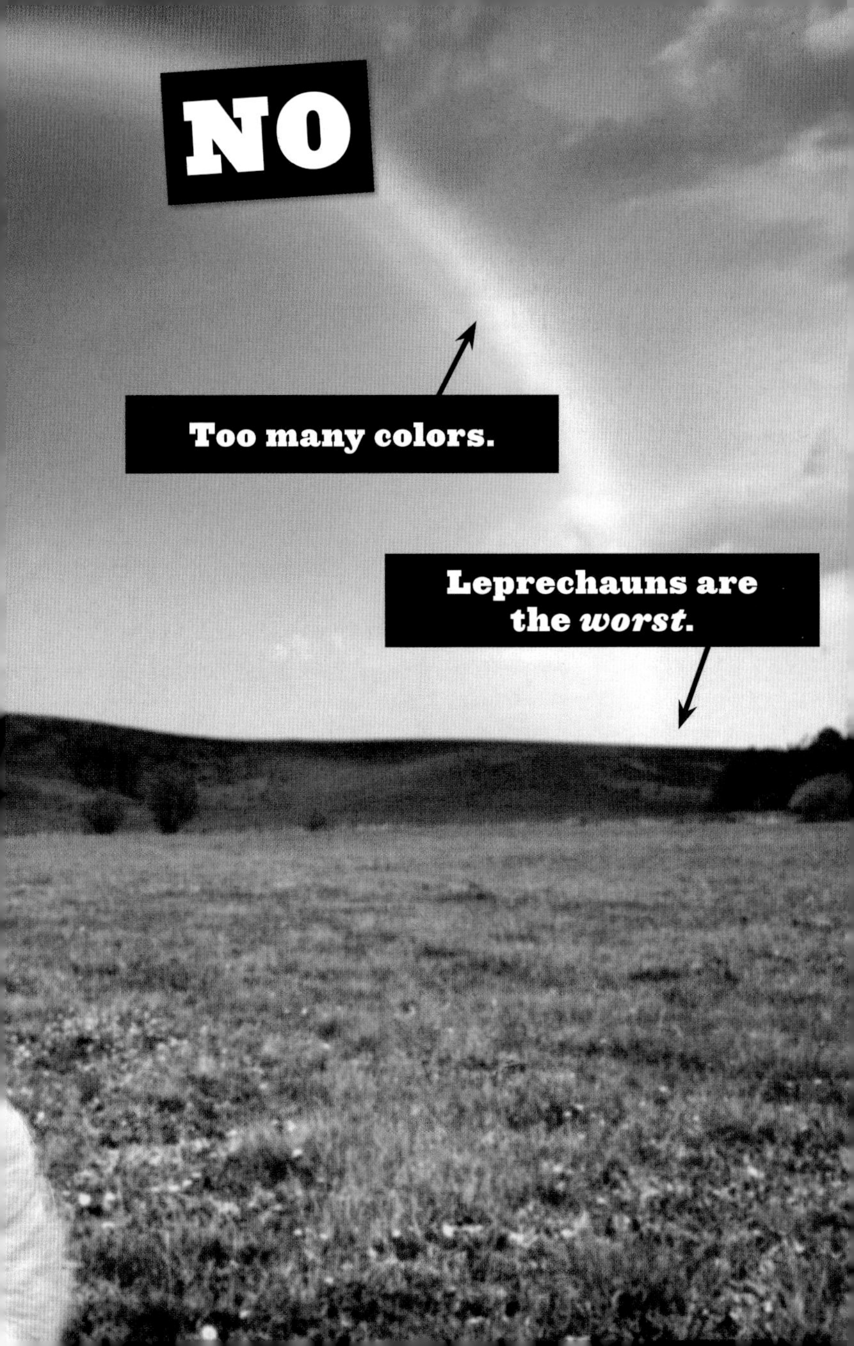
NO
Too many colors.
Leprechauns are the *worst*.

Big Finishes

N

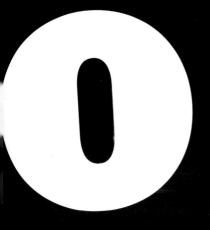

NEVER SAY GOODBYE.

THE SAME GOES FOR HELLO.

NO THE WORLD

**SPREAD THE GRUMP
IN THREE EASY STEPS:**

1 **FIND SOMETHING YOU DON'T LIKE.**

2 **PUT A NO STICKER ON IT.**

3 **REPEAT.**

**(BONUS POINTS IF YOU HIDE AND
THEN THROW THINGS AT PEOPLE
WHO STOP TO READ YOUR STICKER.)**